BRISTOL PUBS

JAMES MACVEIGH

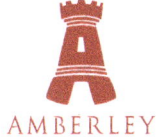

For my family, Marenella, Frankie & Maria.

First published 2017

Amberley Publishing
The Hill, Stroud
Gloucestershire, GL5 4EP

www.amberley-books.com

Copyright © James MacVeigh, 2017
Maps contain Ornance Survey data.
Crown Copyright and database right, 2015

The right of James MacVeigh to be identified
as the Author of this work has been asserted in
accordance with the Copyrights, Designs and
Patents Act 1988.

ISBN 978 1 4456 6168 1 (print)
ISBN 978 1 4456 6169 8 (ebook)

All rights reserved. No part of this book may be
reprinted or reproduced or utilised in any form
or by any electronic, mechanical or other means,
now known or hereafter invented, including
photocopying and recording, or in any information
storage or retrieval system, without the permission
in writing from the Publishers.

British Library Cataloguing in Publication Data.
A catalogue record for this book is available from
the British Library.

Origination by Amberley Publishing.
Printed in the UK.

Contents

	Map	4
	Key	5
	Introduction	6
1	Central	7
2	North	44
3	South	55
4	East	68
5	West	79
	Acknowledgements	96

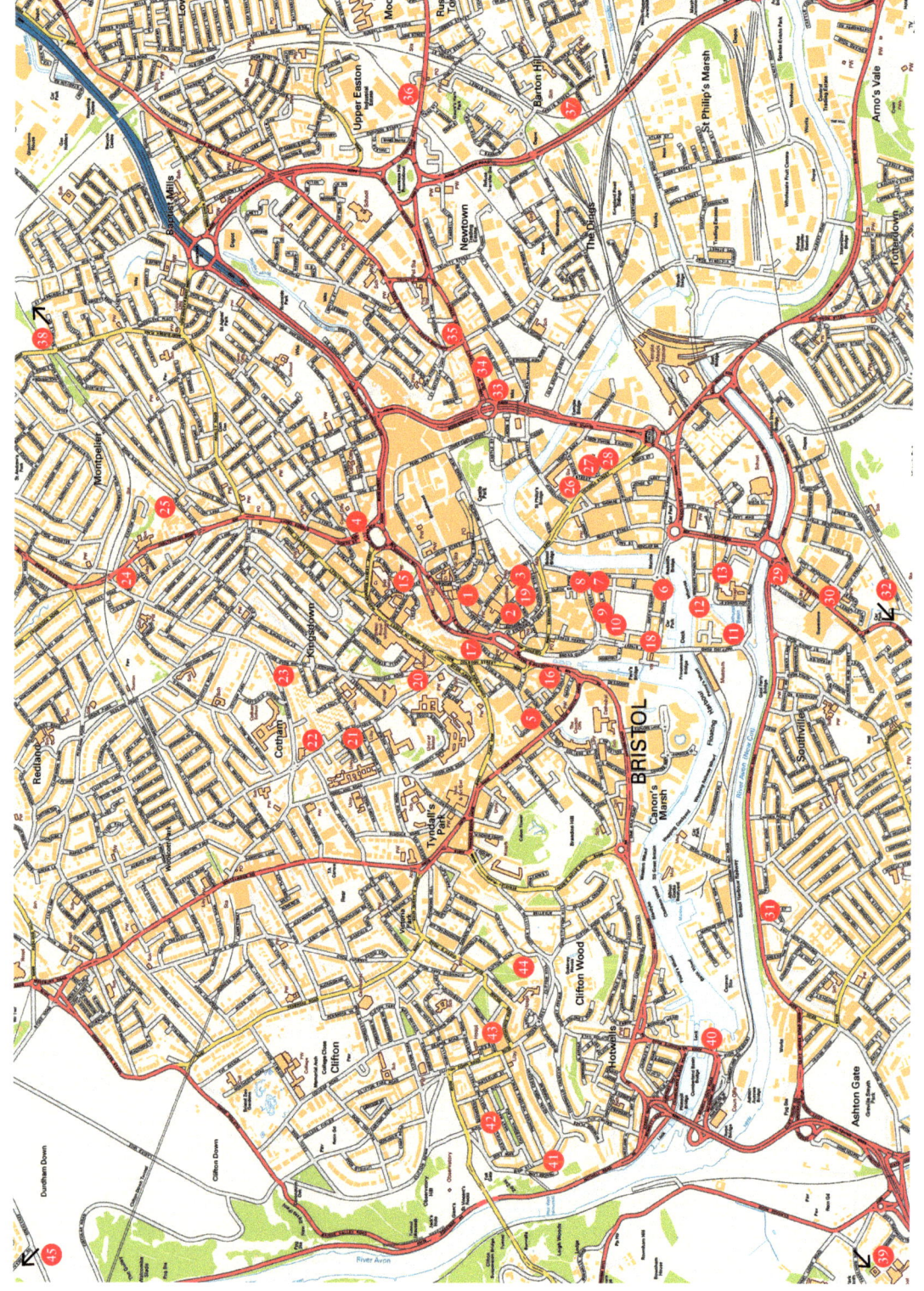

Key

Central
1. The Bank Tavern
2. The Commercial Rooms
3. The Rummer
4. The Full Moon
5. The Hatchet
6. The Hole in the Wall
7. The Llandoger Trow
8. The Old Duke
9. The Famous Royal Navy Volunteer
10. The King William Ale House
11. Louisiana
12. The Ostrich
13. The Golden Guinea
14. The Seven Stars
15. The White Hart
16. The Drawbridge
17. The Christmas Steps
18. The Shakespeare Tavern
19. The Boardroom

North
20. The Colston Arms
21. The White Bear
22. The Highbury Vaults
23. The Cotham Porter Stores
24. The Cat & Wheel
25. The Old England

South
26. The Cornubia
27. The Kings Head
28. Ye Shakespeare
29. The Little Grosvenor
30. The Apple Tree
31. The Avon Packet Tavern
32. The Miners Arms

East
33. The Stag & Hounds
34. The Long Bar
35. The Palace Hotel
36. The Packhorse
37. The Rhubarb Tavern
38. The Farm

West
39. The Angel
40. The Nova Scotia
41. The Avon Gorge Hotel
42. The Coronation Tap
43. The Albion
44. The Lansdown
45. The Lamplighters

Introduction

'There is nothing which has been contrived by Man, by which so much happiness is produced as by a good tavern or inn.'

Dr Samuel Johnson (1709–84)

I decided to write this book because pubs are disappearing with frightening speed. To give just a couple of examples, the Greyhound in Broadwalk has been gobbled up by shops while the Bell, which has been standing in Redcliffe since 1750, is boarded up and derelict. Cheap supermarket booze and the modern world's interest in consulting electronic gadgets rather than going out to socialise have conspired with the need for buildings to convert into flats to make this happen. You have seen this for yourself. Sadly, some of the pubs described in this book will probably be destined for the same fate.

During my research I was surprised by how many of the pubs, often quite ordinary in appearance, had surprising stories to tell and fascinating histories to reveal. For reasons of space I could not include every interesting or historic pub here, so if your local has been omitted, please forgive me, and don't let it stop you from enjoying a journey through the sometimes astonishing history of other public houses in Bristol.

I

Central

1. The Bank Tavern, John Street

Situated in the heart of the old Bristol that once lay within the city walls, the Bank Tavern had an early association with financial institutions, as its name suggests. So far as can be judged from the upper floors of the building, whose style lies firmly in the mid-eighteenth century, the pub was probably erected in or very close to 1750. At the beginning of that year there was no bank in Bristol, although as trade and commerce developed there was a growing need for one. The Bank of England in London had been founded in 1694 at the request of William III as he strove to underwrite the cost of war with France, and by the middle of the century that followed there were twenty banking institutions in the capital, mostly developed by goldsmiths who had both the wealth and the secure premises in which to keep it. The first provincial bank is said to have been opened in Derby, but the evidence for this is hazy. There is no doubt, though, that on 1 August 1750 a bank was opened at the corner of Broad Street and John Street in Bristol, and it seems certain that the Bank Tavern was built soon afterwards to capitalise on the growth of local trade this stimulated.

This will have been considerable, since a contemporary newspaper states, 'The instant deposit of gold was great.' In 1752 a second bank was opened nearby, and four years after that the bank close to the Tavern, having increased in importance, outgrew its Broad Street premises and moved into purpose-built premises on Corn Street, near the junction of Clare Street, where it was known as the Old Bank. That building remains and is still in use as a bank, owned by NatWest.

It would be surprising if no alterations had been made to the Bank Tavern in the more than 250 years since it was built, and the pilasters that frame the windows and doors are a later addition whose style is typically nineteenth century. In the early 1970s new windows were installed on the top floor of the Tavern, and for once the work was carried out so sensitively that the aspect of the building remains unchanged. Unfortunately, the inn sign that hung outside the pub for many years has now gone. The present licensee explained to me that it had fallen into disrepair, and as it would

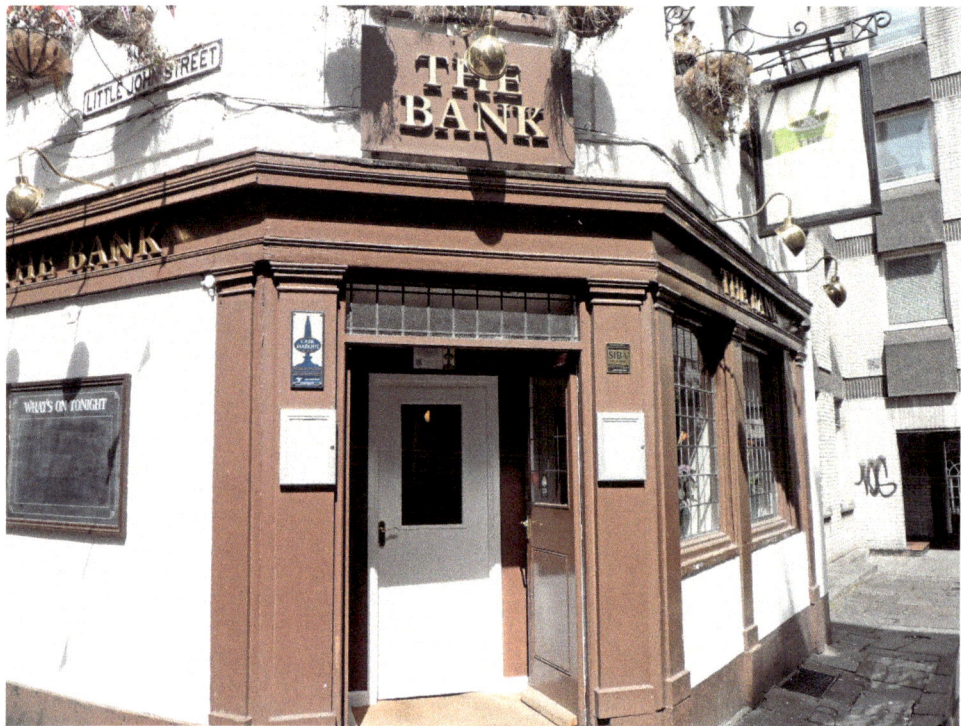

The Bank Tavern.

have cost a small fortune to replace, a new and vastly inferior one was made. Sadly he added, 'Not that it's doing much better.'

The bank that gave birth to the tavern was financed by a consortium of wealthy Bristol merchants including William Miller, a successful grocery wholesaler who lived close by in a Jacobean townhouse known as the Court House, at No. 4 Tailor's Court. A veritable mansion, the house was built by his father, John Miller, and has the first example in Bristol of a shell hood above the front door, bearing its date, 1692. One oddity is that his initials, also carved into the hood, appear clearly as 'I. F. M.' instead of the 'J. F. M.' you would expect. Tragically (some would say criminally), although this wonderful building stands in what would be a prime location for a hotel or conference centre, it stands empty and neglected and is slowly approaching dereliction. Across the road at the old Merchant Tailors' Guild Hall there is another very fine shell hood, which is outstandingly ornate and colourful.

During the Bristol Riots of 1831, with arson rife in the area, the landlord of the Bank Tavern, the aptly named Mr Merry, was disturbed by a group of insurgents who hammered at the door, demanding that he let them in and give them free booze. His refusal was met by the sound of glass breaking as they stove in a fanlight, and when one of the four rioters shouted, 'Let us in or we'll burn the place down!' Mr Merry had no choice but to relent. They polished off three pints of rum before they departed, leaving him – and his tavern – in peace once more.

Above: The Old Bank.

Below: Tailors' Guild shell hood.

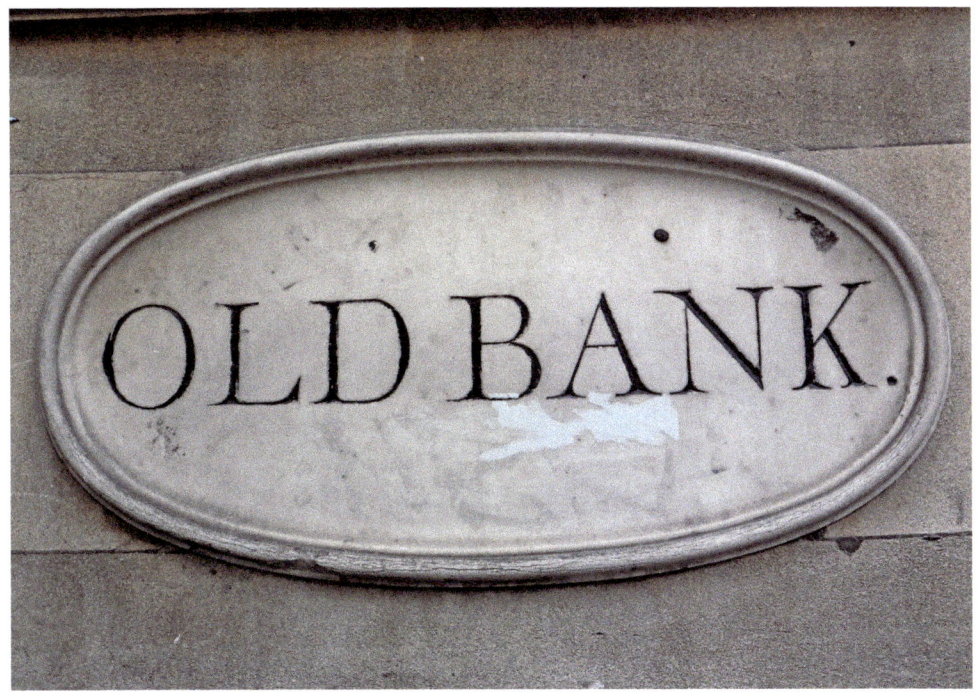

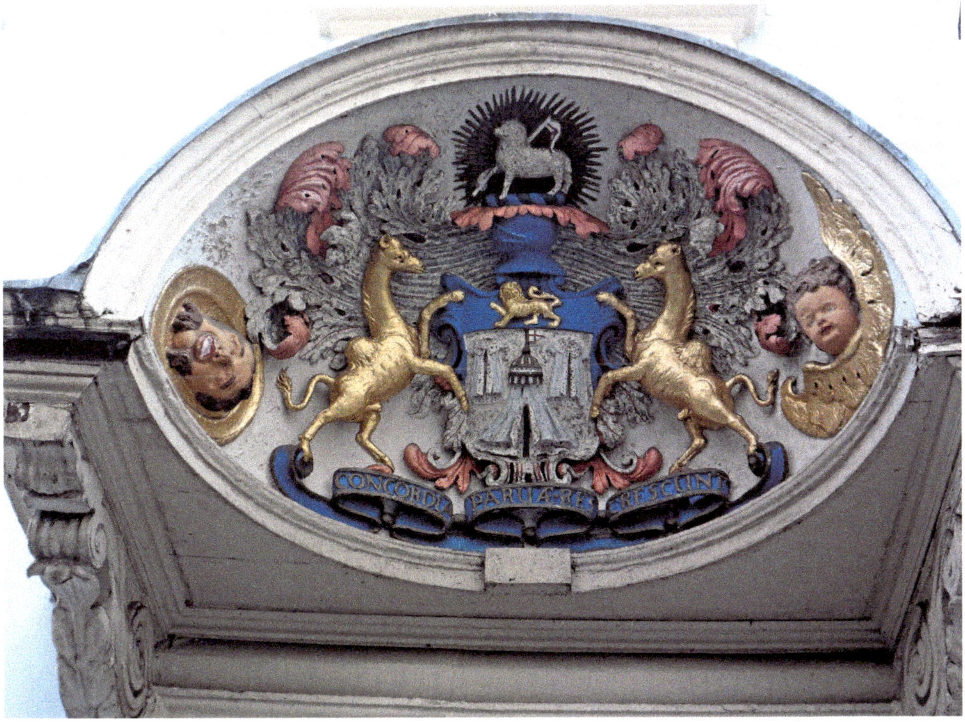

2. The Commercial Rooms, Corn Street

During the late Georgian period, the favourite haunt of Bristol merchants where they could discuss their deals was Foster's Coffee House in Corn Street. They must have recovered well from the abolition of the slave trade in 1807 because soon afterwards they commissioned a London architect, Charles Busby, to replace it with a new building on the same site. Finished in 1810, the Commercial Rooms he designed was a version of the Liverpool merchants' Lyceum building, but on a more modest scale. As someone familiar with both structures, I have to say that I find the Bristol building better proportioned and more elegant. The sculptor, J. G. Bubb, flushed with success after decorating John Nash's development of terraces around Regent's Park, created the figures portraying Bristol, Commerce, and Navigation above the stone portico, each with the long neck that is characteristic of his work. There is also a frieze that depicts Neptune offering all parts of the world to Britannia that is typical of the imperial thinking of the time. In the early years, the merchants held their meetings on an upstairs floor, lit by a circular leaded light over 9 metres (30 feet) in diameter and crowned by a glass dome held up by twelve caryatids – pillars in female form.

At some point, the merchants' loose assembly became formalised as a gentleman's club, the Clifton Club, and in 1856 the club moved to an even more grandiose building in the Mall in Clifton, where it remains to this day. For some time afterwards the Commercial Rooms became notorious as a haunt of prostitutes. Remnants of the club remained, though,

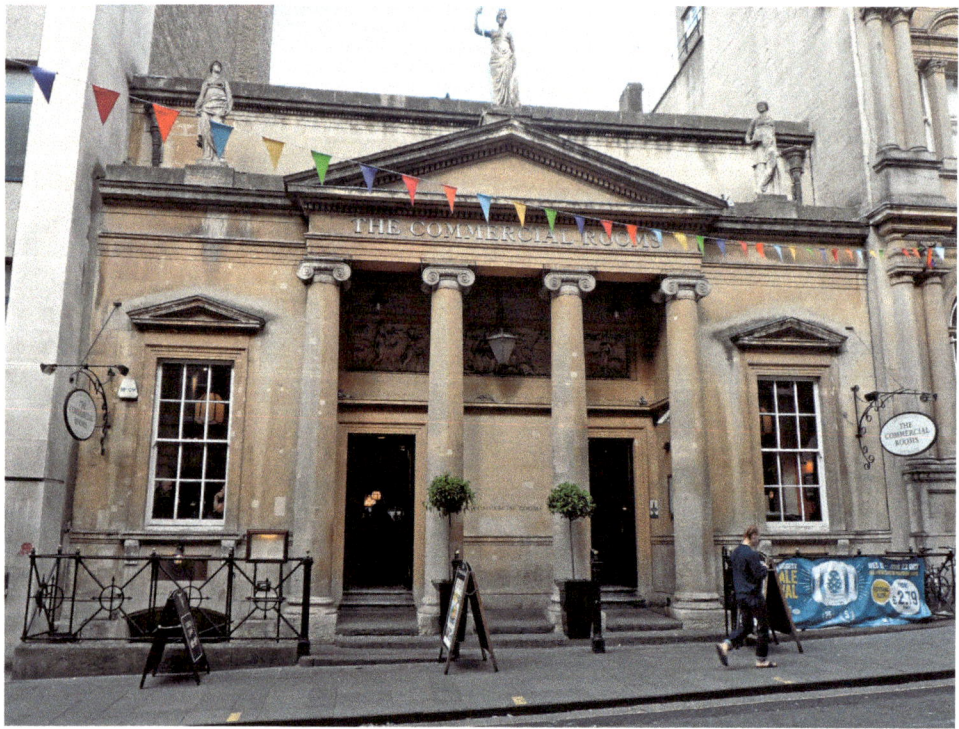

The Commercial Rooms.

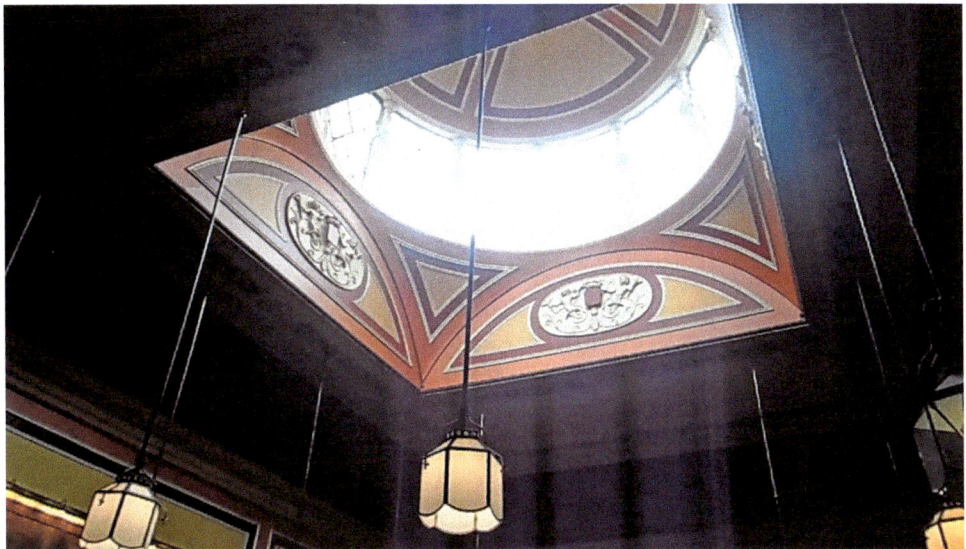

A magnificent fanlight.

and a gentleman's club survived in the Rooms until the 1990s when, desperate because of lack of support, they reluctantly allowed women to become members. This did not save them, however, and the building was sold to the JD Wetherspoons chain, who transformed it into the successful pub it is today. At an unknown time in the past the upper floor was removed, so that today's customers enjoy their refreshments under a magnificent fanlight, making the Commercial Rooms probably the only drinking establishment in the UK, and perhaps the world, to possess such a feature. Keen to retain the building's links with the past, Wetherspoons also retained the weathervane above the bar, which let Georgian merchants know when it was safe for their ships to navigate the often turbulent waters of the Avon Gorge. There are also wall boards inscribed with the names of former club officials.

Many people have never noticed it, but there is a cocktail bar and restaurant in the Commercial Rooms' basement. Called the Ox and famous for its steaks, it is said to be a favourite rendezvous for adulterous couples.

3. The Rummer, All Saints' Lane

No book about Bristol pubs would be complete without mentioning the Rummer. Even though at the time of writing only the hotel part of the establishment is in use, the bars and restaurant are open to passers-by. The name refers to a large vessel for shared drinking, and one made of copper that is kept at the hotel may once have been its inn sign. The Rummer occupies the site of what was probably Bristol's very first inn, parts of which remain in its medieval cellars. The tavern, which began life as the Green Lattis, is first mentioned in 1241, which with its closeness to the bridge that gave the city its name – first Brycgstowe, 'the place of the bridge', worn down to Brigstow and finally Bristol – gives this claim validity. All Saints' Lane came into existence when the architect John Wood built the Exchange in 1743. Formerly known as Venney's Lane,

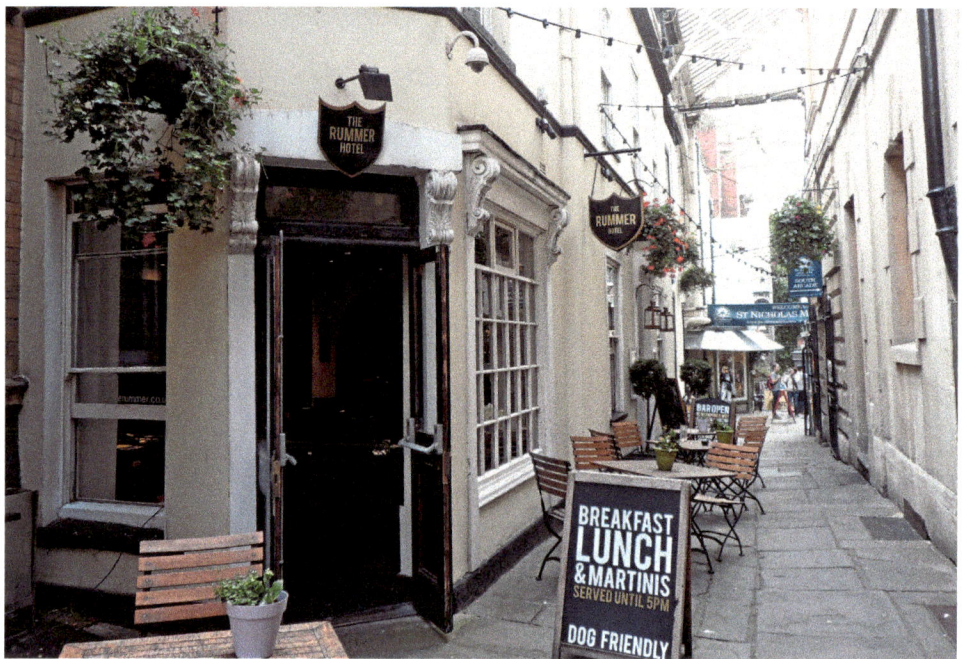

The Rummer.

it had been the site of the inn's extensive stables when the Rummer became Bristol's terminus for the London mail coach in 1784, at which time its entrance was in the High Street. The arrival of the railway killed off this trade and the last four-horse stagecoach rolled up to the pub in 1843.

During the English Civil War the inn was occupied first by Cavaliers, then by Roundheads, and Oliver Cromwell was recorded as staying there in 1646 'on his way to govern Ireland according to his Irish ideas', which included fixing hats made of pitch onto people's heads in the town of Drogheda and setting fire to them. Elizabeth I, Charles I and William III are all said to have stayed at the Rummer during visits to Bristol.

One of the most bizarre taxes ever introduced was one of 5s put on all privately owned watches and clocks in 1797. People stopped using them and relied instead on the so-called Parliamentary Clocks in public places. The Rummer possesses a fine example of one that is actually dated earlier, around 1780.

The present manager has plans to reopen the Rummer pub via its High Street entrance.

4. The Full Moon, Stokes Croft

The Full Moon at the bottom of Stokes Croft has often looked rather forlorn and neglected in the past, standing as it does at one of the main gateways into Bristol but dwarfed by office blocks and behind a busy highway. In fact it is ancient, and not only that, it was built on the site of an even older inn that was probably only the second to appear in Bristol. According to the city's historian Samuel Seyer (1757–1831), who

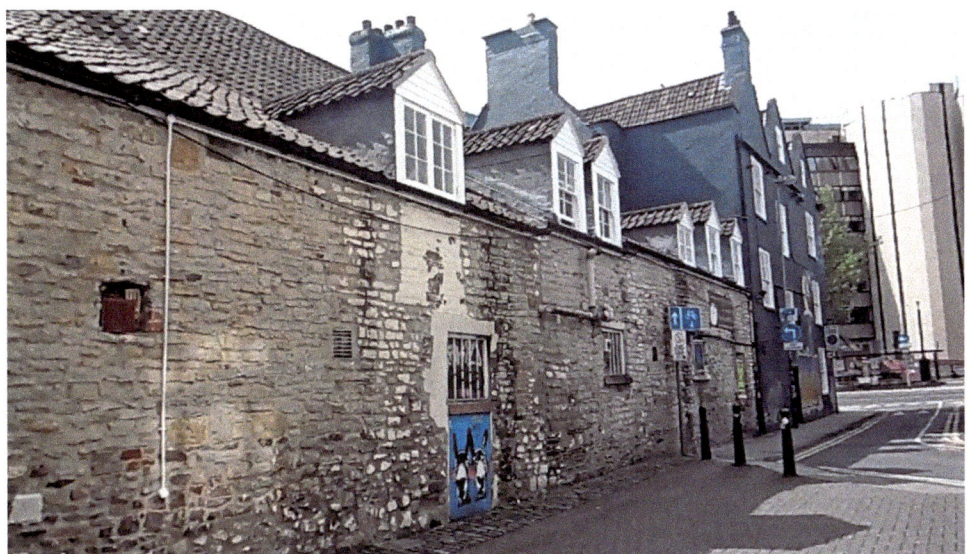

The oldest part of the Full Moon.

used ancient documents to create a map of Old Bristol as it was in 1250–1350, the spot was occupied even then by 'the Full Moon, a very Ancient Hostellerie'. It is a refreshing fact that the pub has never changed its name, but there may be some doubt about Seyer's map as he was refused access to original documents in the Bristol council house, and had to base his conclusions on manuscripts in Oxford's Bodleian Library. Be that as it may, the building is now listed as being 'of special architectural interest'.

Until its recent paint job, when local artists were recruited to decorate the Full Moon's outside walls with galaxies of stars, the modern pub was in many ways an edgy place – on the edge of St Paul's, on the edge of town – but this merely repeats its history: in the early eighteenth century the inn was close to the edge of the old Bristol city boundary with Gloucestershire. Old inns can be as adaptable as the human beings who created them, and the Full Moon has recently gained a new lease of life. Taking advantage of its closeness to Bristol bus station, it has reinvented itself as a backpacker hostel for the many youngsters who visit the city from home and abroad. This has brought more customers to its bars and given it the impetus to start up as a busy music venue.

Take a closer look, and you will recognise the building for the old coaching inn it is. If you walk the short distance up little Moon Street beside the inn, you will see that the wall there is made of ancient stonework, while the dormer windows that light the bedrooms date from the seventeenth century, and the gables above them are Jacobean. The rest of the pub is around a century younger, mainly rebuilt in the 1700s, than the additions tacked on during Victorian times and later. The date of the stupendous iron archway, the work of a local smith, is unknown: it may or may not be merely coincidence that Simon Shilstone, the innkeeper from 1776–93, was also a blacksmith. At around his time both the fields that bordered the Full Moon and the inn's stable yard were favourite locations for bare-knuckle prize fights between both men and women. Female pugilists were by no

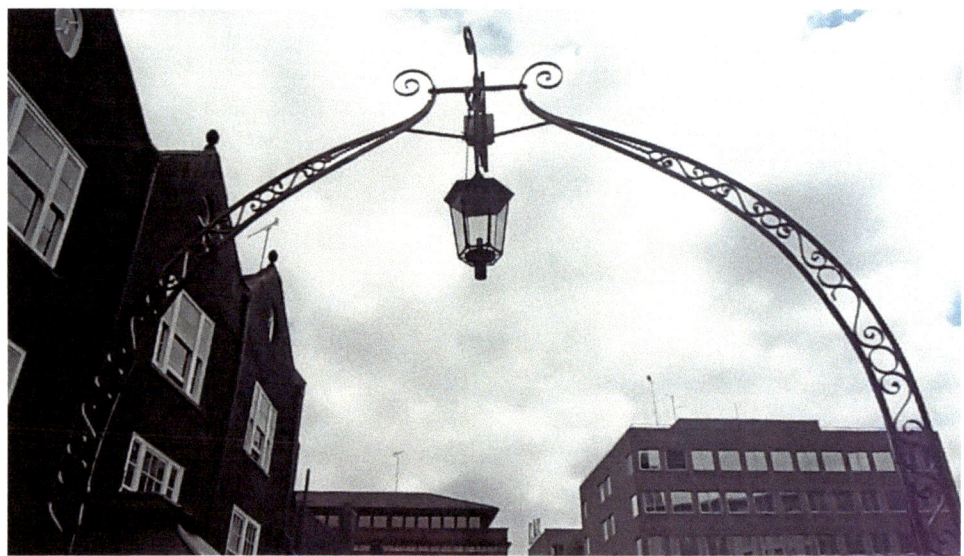

Above: The Full Moon's arch.

Below: Drunkard's staircase.

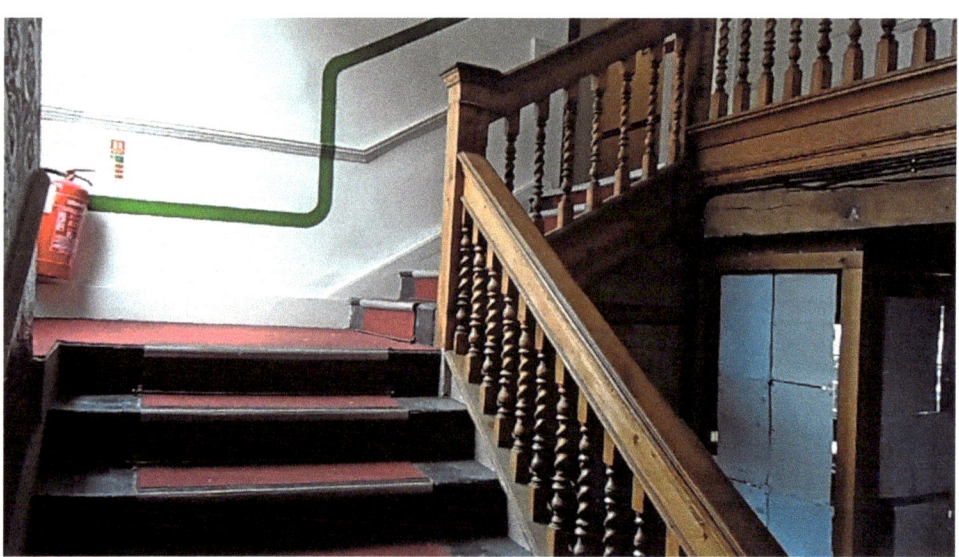

means rare. Earlier in the eighteenth century, in May 1728, the Bristol boxer Moll Buck fought her London rival, Mary Barker, for a purse of 7 guineas at the Green Dragon inn on St Michael's Hill. The result of the contest is not known.

A later extension to the Full Moon is the portico outside the main entrance, erected to protect visitors from bad weather as they arrived or left by coach. This is the kind of structure only seen these days on Christmas cards, and like iron arch you pass under to see it, it is the only example of its type in Bristol. Inside the pub the most remarkable feature is its 'drunkard's staircase', which leads from the bar to the bedrooms above. Like the wall to its left this is a remnant of the seventeenth-century inn, and it earned its name because of its structure. Wide enough for two relatively sober men to support a third who is dead drunk on his way upstairs, the stairs treads are 28 cm (11 inches) from front to back and rise by only 15 cm (6 inches), so that the going is made easy. In 1942 this remarkable relic of an earlier time was described as, 'so covered by paint and varnish that it is difficult to ascertain the nature of the wood'. Fortunately, when Courages brewery renovated the pub in the mid-1970s they had the good sense to restore the staircase. Like the iron arch outside, it now has a preservation order upon it so that, thankfully, it can never be removed, defaced or altered.

5. The Hatchet, Frogmore Street

A short walk from the city centre, along Denmark Street to the left of the Bristol Hippodrome, brings the walker face to face with the ancient Hatchet Inn, a Grade II-listed building. The name is curious, perhaps unique, and it would be impossible to guess its origin by merely standing outside the pub today. Not only is it probable that William Shakespeare was still in his boyhood when parts of the building were constructed, it is possible that he had not even been born as there is evidence that the Hatchet was built onto a fifteenth-century farmhouse. If anything of the original survives it will be deep within the present walls or foundations, and the date '1606' on its front wall most likely harks back to when it was first licensed as an inn.

At that time, Clifton was a remote and secluded village. The pedestrians, horse riders and country carts that had to visit it travelled up Frog Lane (a forerunner of today's Frogmore Street) to do so, and the desire of this traffic for a pause before tackling the hill was probably what brought the inn into existence. At a time when Park Street had not yet been built and Leigh Woods extended all the way down to Frog Lane, there is little doubt that the Hatchet was a favourite watering hole with the foresters who worked there. They brought the tools of their trade with them when they stopped off for a drink on their way home from work, and this is how the inn gained its unusual name. When Alderman Day was granted land to develop Park Street in 1740, he named the new street after an area of dairy farmland it crossed, Bullock's Park, and the Hatchet became sidelined.

The original inn was smaller than the present building but had a well, stables, a cockpit, outbuildings and a large stable yard of which a small, cobbled area still remains. One half-timbered outbuilding survived into the 1940s, when it was destroyed by a firebomb in the Second World War. In the early 1960s, Mecca received planning permission for a new Entertainment Centre on Frogmore Street and the road layout was altered to accommodate the Ford Prefects, Triumph Heralds and Morris Oxfords that would flock there. There were even plans to demolish the Hatchet, and when these were resisted it ended up on the traffic island where it stands today. Perhaps as a compensation for the land it lost, in 1967 the houses on its either side were added to the Hatchet as extensions.

There is a myth that the Hatchet's yard was once the venue for bare-knuckle boxing, like the Full Moon, but it was too out of the way for that. The story probably arose because it was frequented by bare-knuckle fighters who made their name in London like Tom Cribb, who was born in Lawrence Hill in 1871 and grew up in Hanham. There is

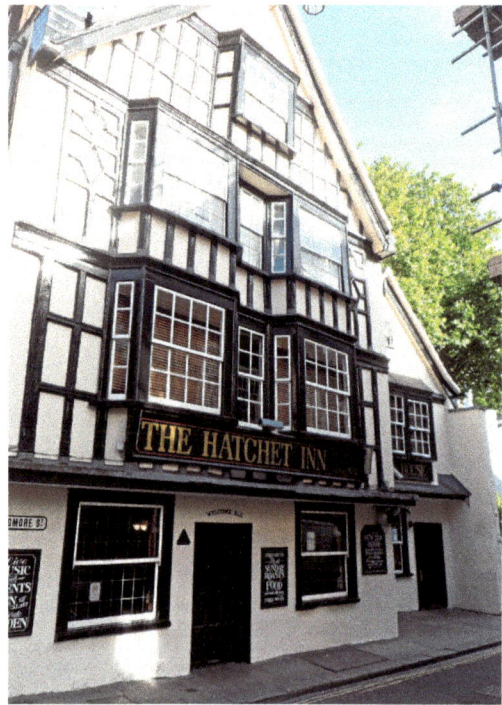
The Hatchet.

a pub called the Tom Cribb in the capital's theatre land with a blue plaque outside to remember him; Cribb was actually the licensee of that pub, then called the Union and slap-bang in the middle of a red-light area, when he retired from the ring. Other pugilists who patronised the Hatchet were Mike Tyston's hero Jem Mace, born in Norfolk in 1831 and known as the Gypsy. The Brighton bricklayer pugilist, Tom Sayers, born in 1826, also patronised the Hatchet. Sayers was the last of the famous bare-knuckle fighters, as well as the world's first heavyweight boxing champion. His most famous illegal bout lasted two hours and twenty-seven minutes and its spectators included Charles Dickens, William Makepeace Thackeray and the then prime minister, Lord Palmerston.

In the eighteenth century the Hatchet had a rat pit at its rear, which had a whitewashed base. To take part in this 'sport' men would bring their terrier dogs to the pub, a large numbers of rats would be put into the pit, bets would be laid as to which dog would kill the most in a specified time, and the dogs would be dropped in. This activity may have continued at the Hatchet for around a century.

The Hatchet's entrance door is centuries old but no less sturdy for that, its twelve panels are heavily studded and surrounded by a frame that may be oak.

6. The Hole in the Wall, the Grove

This dockside tavern has two features that make it unique. The first is a tiny room, around 1 square metre, which juts out from the main building on the side of its original waterside entrance, below the inn sign that the Beefeater chain erected when they took over the pub. It was probably due to this little construction, known as the spy house, that the inn gained its name. Observation slits built into its walls gave commanding views both ways along the dock and allowed drinkers to keep a watch for marauding press gangs, at a time when the term meant something even more sinister than roaming packs of paparazzi. The inn is thought to have been built around 1700, and for much of the ensuing century it was common for Royal Navy press gangs to prowl the area in search of unwilling recruits. Their prime targets were drunken sailors, although they were not above taking innocent landlubbers when it suited them. They would overpower their victim, drag him aboard a navy ship and imprison him until they were out at sea, when he would have no choice but to enrol as a seaman. A constant watch was maintained from the spy house, and if pressmen were spotted customers would beat a hasty exit through a back door leading into a passage that came out in Queen Square.

Given the Hole in the Wall's dockside location, it would be astonishing if some of its customers at that time were not smugglers, and they would have used the spy house to keep a weather eye open for the Excise men based at the Custom House on the far side of Queen Square. Built in 1711, that building was destroyed in the Bristol Riot of 1831 and replaced six years later by the present Custom House, designed by Sidney Smirke (1798–1877). This gifted architect also designed the Bethlehem Royal Hospital in London, better known as Bedlam, which is now the Imperial War Museum.

The second thing that makes the Hole in the Wall unique is the probable truth of its claim to have been the model for the Spy-Glass Inn in Robert Louis Stevenson's classic, *Treasure Island*. The circumstantial evidence for this is convincing. The book's hero, young Jim Hawkins, sets out on his search for buried treasure by going to Bristol to

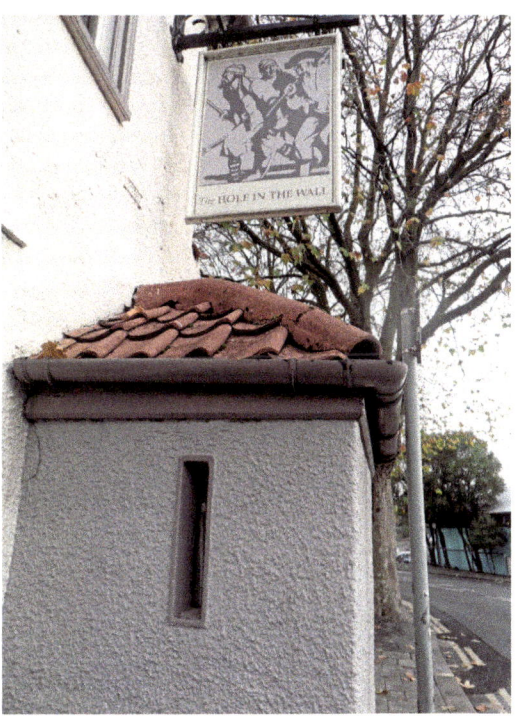

The Hole in the Wall spy house.

join the good ship *Hispaniola,* and finds the Spy-Glass 'by following the line of the docks…' The thing that clinches the Hole in the Wall's claim, at least for your author, is Stevenson's description, 'There was a street on each side, and an open door on both, which made the long, low room pretty clear to see in, in spite of clouds of tobacco smoke.' All right, the tobacco has now been banned and Long John Silver is no longer the landlord seen by Jim Hawkins, 'propped on his crutch' at the bar, but the long, low room remains as does the open door to a street on either side.

Whatever the veracity of the Hole in the Wall's claim, it is certainly believed by one small but very active Bristol charity, the Long John Silver Trust. On the green outside the pub visitors may notice a palm tree in an old wooden wine barrel. A series of these form the Trust's Treasure Island Trail around Bristol's ancient port, which begins in King Street with the one pictured below. The charity has a long-term plan to erect a statue of Long John Silver on the green by the Hole in the Wall, where it would be enjoyed by tourists and locals alike and be an asset to Bristol. The Treasure Island Trail is well worth following, and even lifelong Bristol residents will be sure to learn new things if they do so.

The Hole in the Wall is an unusual name for an inn but it is not unique, there are pubs of that name in Torquay and Nottingham, and another in Cambridgeshire was recently renamed. The Bristol inn was originally called the Coach & Horses but was often referred to as the Hole in the Wall in ancient times. The name usually refers to a breach in a boundary and it is no surprise that inns of that name appeared in Prince Street, which lay just outside the walls of the medieval city of Bristol. The first Hole in the Wall

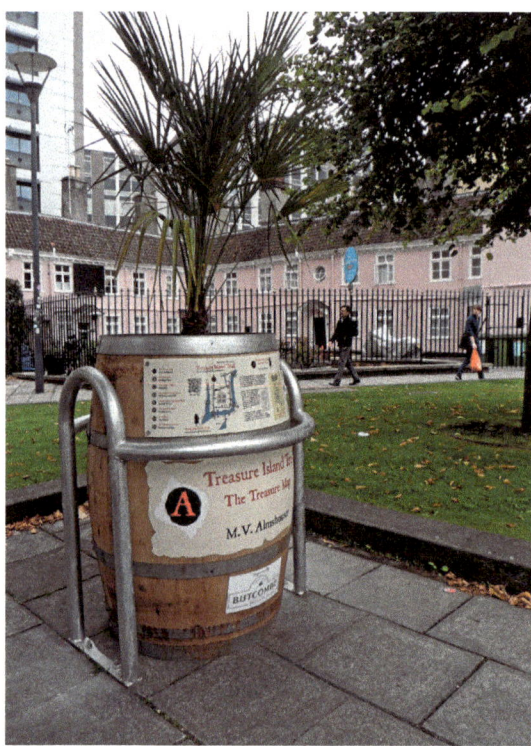

Treasure Island Trail.

there may have changed its name later to the Shipwrights Arms or that may have been its official title, but little more is known about it. A later Hole in the Wall, built on or near the site now occupied by the Prince Street/King Street roundabout, later became known as the Merchants Arms and was one of those attacked by 'gangs of twenty men or so' demanding free booze during the Bristol Riot in 1831. The landlord at the time was probably one Robert Smart, if so the event must have affected him badly because he put it up for sale the following year. Ownership of the inn passed to Bristol Corporation when its lease expired in 1874; in addition to the inn, the property included an adjoining house in King Street as well as small shop with a slaughterhouse behind it.

Sadly, the phenomenon where people, all men so far as I know, leave pubs the worse for drink only to fall into one of Bristol's waterways and drown, is not a new one. In the 1840s, the Humane Society furnished the Hole in the Wall with 'Hooks and Drags for speedily withdrawing persons, in danger of being drowned, out of the water.' Most of the other dockside pubs named in this book were also given them.

7. The Llandoger Trow, King Street

Like King Street where it stands, the Llandoger Trow pub is distinctive and quirky, both architecturally and in the richness of its history. Even its name is unique. It first appeared around 1664 when a Captain Hawkins gave up his command of a trow (the kind of flat-bottomed boat Bristol used at the time to trade with Welsh ports), bought No. 5 King Street and converted it to an inn, which he named after his home village, Llandogo. When the Berni Inns pub chain took it over in 1962 the Llandoger Trow had been an established inn for almost three centuries, originally as one of a row of five imposing, half-timbered, four-storey houses. Nos 1 and 2 had been destroyed in the Blitz but the Berni brothers bought the two remaining historic buildings, Nos 3 and 4 King Street, and made them into one large pub-restaurant beside the harbour of Welsh Back, so called because the merchants' houses that had stood there in Captain Hawkins' time, which were also their warehouses, backed right onto the quay. The Llandoger building was dilapidated. It might have collapsed, as many of Bristol's other ancient buildings were allowed to do, but the Berni brothers had reinforced posts more than 13 metres long driven into the ground and used the original timbers to rebuild the old inn around them in a refurbishment sensitive to the past. They even kept a dip of 20 cm between the centre and the outer edges of the upstairs floors, retaining the ancient feel of the place.

The style of the Llandoger, with its splendid half-timbered frontage and overhanging eaves, reminds the visitor of Tudor buildings. Its original houses were put to many different uses over the centuries, including occupation as dwellings, by a gunsmith, a separate inn called the Goat, a tobacconist and a wholesale grocer. Some owners altered windows while one created a shopfront, which gives the building an eccentric, higgledy-piggledy aspect that is pleasing to the eye. The lamp above the front door is a reproduction, but the bracket that holds it is authentic, a reminder of the days when there were no street lights. During the Berni Inns refurb, seven plastered-over fireplaces were revealed, and there can be few better places to take a drink on a winter's night than on a leather sofa beside one of their blazing log fires. The oak staircase leading

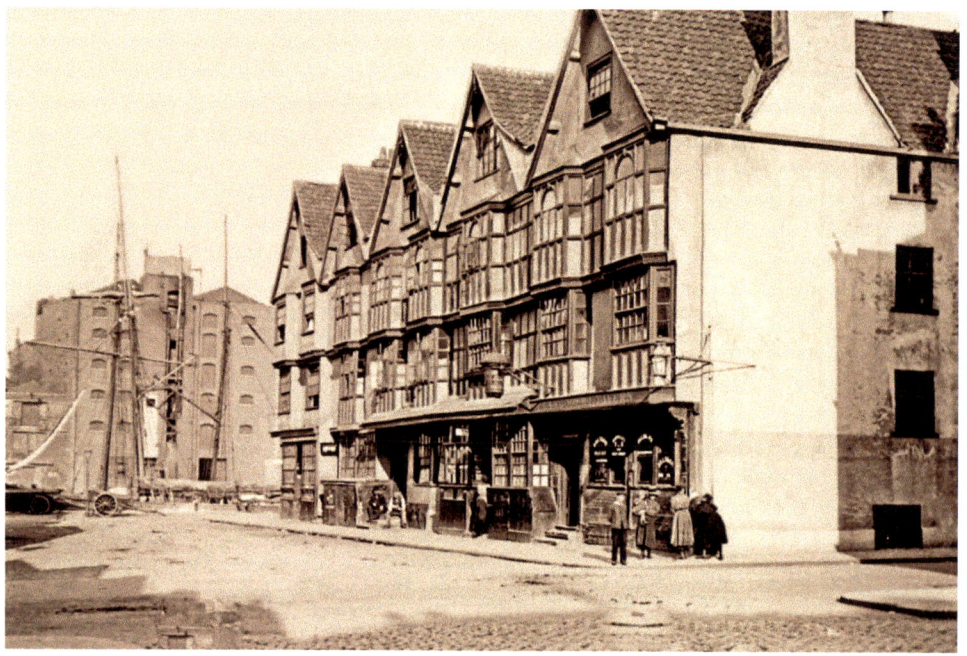

Above: The Llandoger in the 1880s...

Below: ...and now.

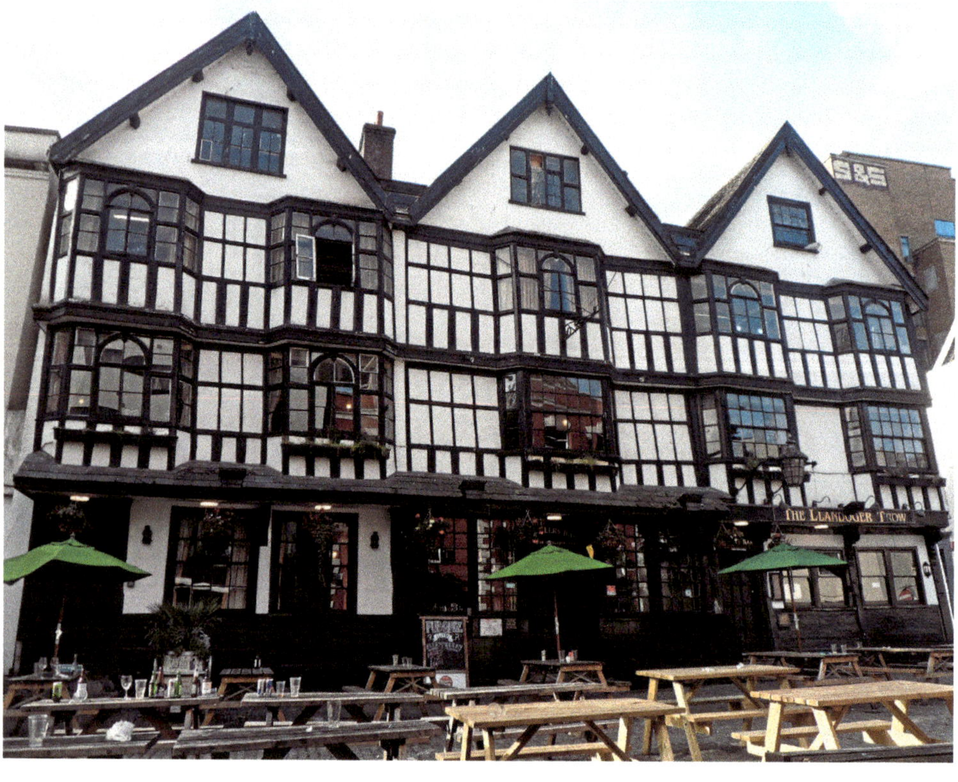

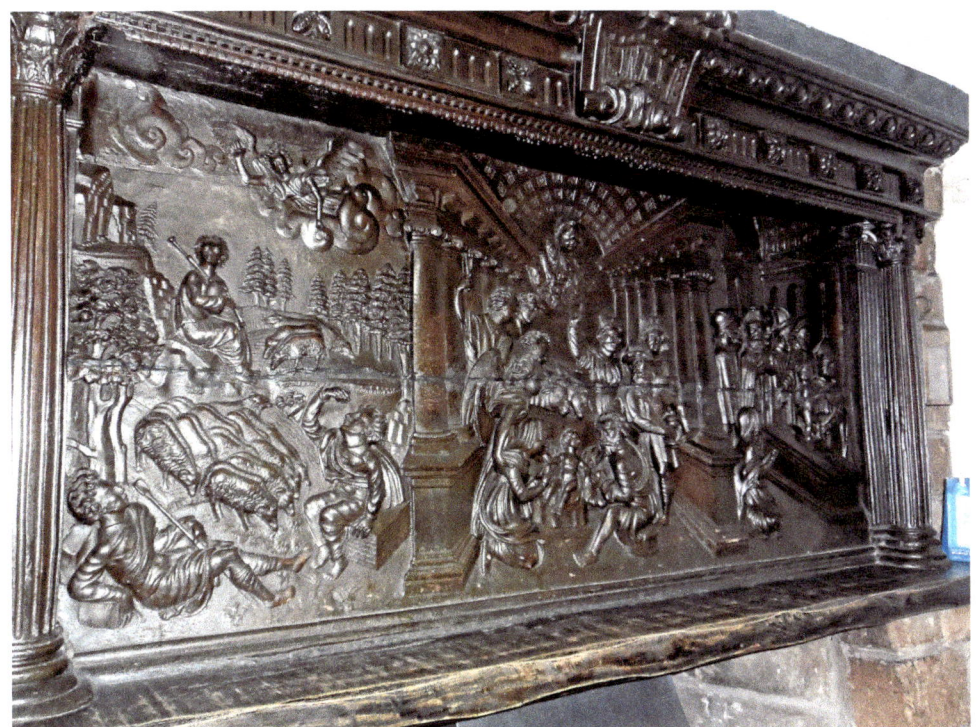

Seven fireplaces were uncovered.

to the upper floors is original and unspoilt, with newels, handrails and balusters in wonderful condition, and although squeezed into a small space the rise is fairly gentle as there are three flights to each floor. A black ceiling in one of the bars is accounted for with a story that it was once decorated with paintings of naked ladies, and that a landlady whose allurements were ignored as seafarers looked upwards had it painted over. It is hard to see how paintings would have fitted in with the plasterwork, but while the ceiling remains black the story is impossible to disprove.

Along with its elegant neighbour, Queen Square, King Street is one of the best-preserved remnants of old Bristol to survive the Second World War. It was created in 1650 when conditions in cramped, overcrowded, unsanitary old Bristol, whose buildings were mainly built of timber, became intolerable and wealthy merchants decided to move beyond the city's southern wall. Up until that time the area had been the old Town Marsh, of which nothing remains today but a distant memory in the name of nondescript Marsh Street. A place where sheep grazed and rubbish was dumped, the Marsh was also the venue for 'entertainments' such as bear-baiting and the occasional execution by hanging of pirates, before the latter were transferred to London's infamous Execution Dock. The oldest building in King Street, the Grade II-listed St Nicholas' almshouses on the opposite side to the Llandoger Tow, was erected in 1652–54. Its interior was completely destroyed in the Blitz but the façade was restored in 1961 and now houses private apartments.

Maritime and literary legends abound at the Llandoger, and some fall into both of these categories. There have been claims in the past that the stone flags in the main bar were once crossed by Robert Louis Stevenson, and even that the tavern was the model for the Spy-Glass Inn in his timeless classic, *Treasure Island*, though as stated earlier this accolade is generally reserved for the Hole in the Wall on the far side of Queen Square. Other associations with the book may be authentic. The Llandoger Trow lays claim to having been the inspiration for the Admiral Benbow, Jim Hawkins' boyhood home, and the fact that 'Jim lad' shares a surname with the Bristol pub's first landlord may give the idea some credence.

Another alleged literary and nautical connection is the story that Daniel Defoe met Alexander Selkirk, or Selcraig, the model for his eponymous hero in *Robinson Crusoe*, at the Llandoger. There is no way of proving or disproving this conclusively, though the two men *were* in Bristol at the same time, staying at separate inns in Cock and Bottle Lane where Defoe was a so-called Sunday Gentleman, hiding from creditors and only able to leave the Star Inn on the Sabbath when debtors were immune from arrest. By all accounts an objectionable individual, Selkirk was sailing master of the *Cinque Ports*, part of a treasure-seeking expedition under the overall command of William Dampier. In 1704, she dropped anchor off the island of Más a Tierra, 400 miles from the coast of Chile, for repairs, and when Selkirk objected that the ship was too infested with marine worm to put back to sea the ship's captain, Stradling, gave him his sea chest and marooned him on the island. More than four years later he was picked up by another ship in search of Spanish treasure, the *Duke*, part of a flotilla commanded by the Bristol privateer and explorer, Woodes Rogers, who wrote that they had brought aboard, 'a man cloth'd in Goat-Skins, who looked wilder than the first owners of them'. Ironically, this expedition also contained William Dampier, who attested to Selkirk's skill as a seaman, as a result of which he was given command first of a captured ship, later of the *Duke* itself. He returned to his native Scotland a wealthy man but failed to settle; he married bigamously, returned to the sea and eventually died of yellow fever off Guinea on the West African coast.

There can be no doubt that smugglers, buccaneers, pirates and privateers were among the Llandoger Trow's clientele in the seventeenth and eighteenth centuries. Captain Woodes Rogers lived around the corner, literally, at No. 19 Queen Square, and it would be surprising if he and associates like William Dampier, born in the Somerset village of East Coker in 1652, did not habituate the inn. The place may even have been patronised by that most infamous of all pirates, Blackbeard, for although there has always been controversy about his place of birth this was most likely in Redcliffe, a short walk from King Street and the Llandoger Trow. The pub was also frequently used for the recruitment of privateers, the legalised pirates who received a letter of marque from the British government that allowed them to pillage enemy merchantmen when Britain was at war. The advertisement shown is one of many placed in a Bristol newspaper, *Felix Farley's Bristol Journal*, in 1757.

Like many old inns, the Llandoger Trow comes complete with resident ghosts. The oldest and most persistent ghostly legend tells of a spirit in the attic that drags one foot behind the other when it walks, and is said to belong to a boy named Pierre who died in

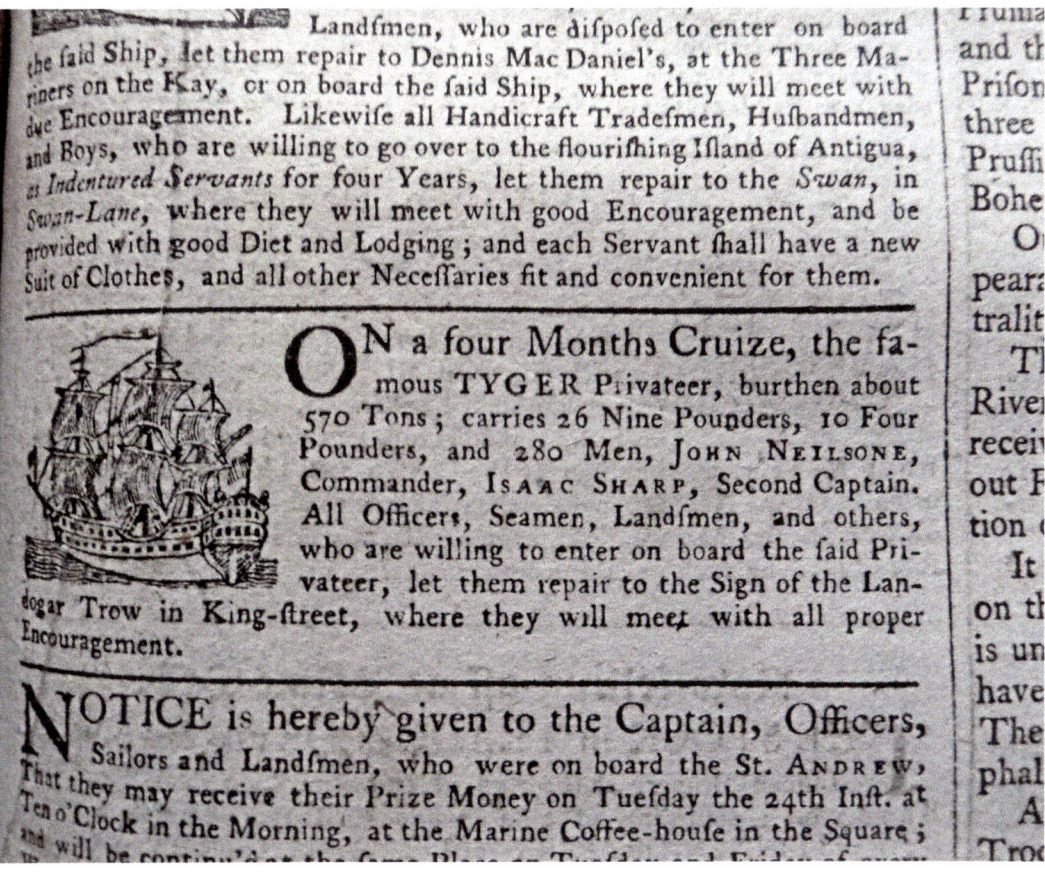

Privateers' Ad.

the pub many years ago. Another story is that on one occasion the staff saw two figures on the pub's CCTV cameras and believed they were customers who had stayed on after closing time, but when they went to investigate the figures had vanished. TV's *Most Haunted* programme spent a night in the Llandoger in 2009 and came to the conclusion that it has at least fifteen resident spirits. According to the programme, one inhabits the old ship's figurehead, which stands beside the beautifully carved fireplace in the Smugglers bar, apparently longing to be set free. Perhaps she does not like to be seen after the accident to her nose, or is just too close to the roaring log fire that makes the pub so cosy in winter.

The Llandoger Trow's is close to the Theatre Royal on the far side of King Street, which was presented with a royal licence by George III giving it the right to display the royal coat of arms, which still holds pride of place on its outer wall. Countless theatrical celebrities have patronised the pub including old stars like Henry Irving, Ellen Terry and Sir Max Beerbohm. There are Theatre Royal posters in the Jacobean Room advertising plays with an entrance fee of 4d – 2p today!

Fascinating though it is, the Llandoger Trow is not the only pub worth visiting in King Street.

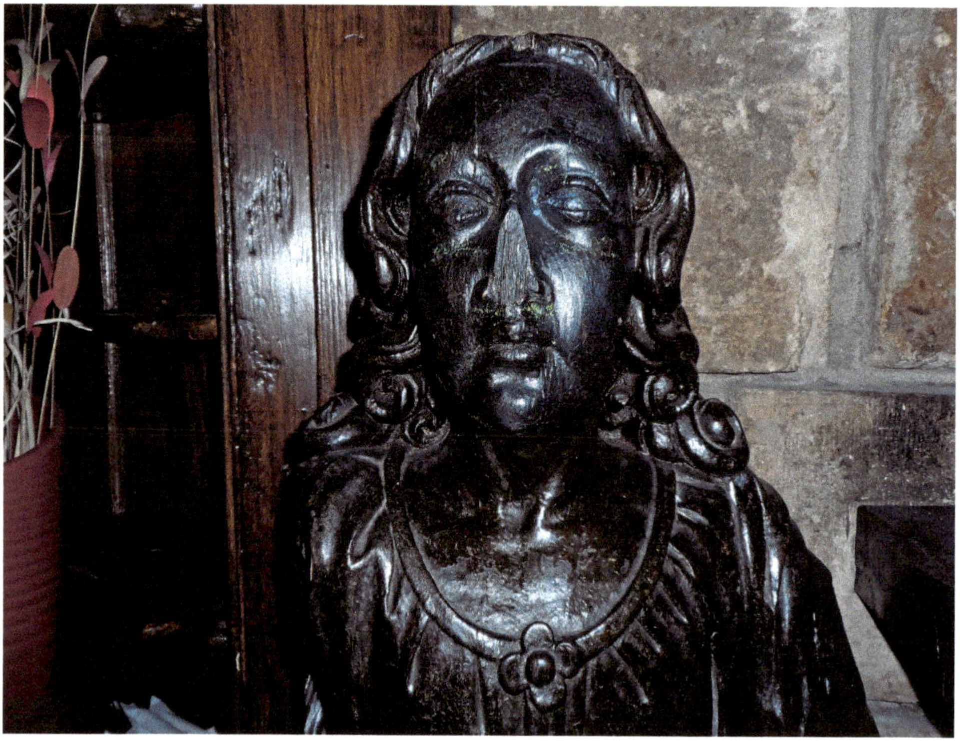

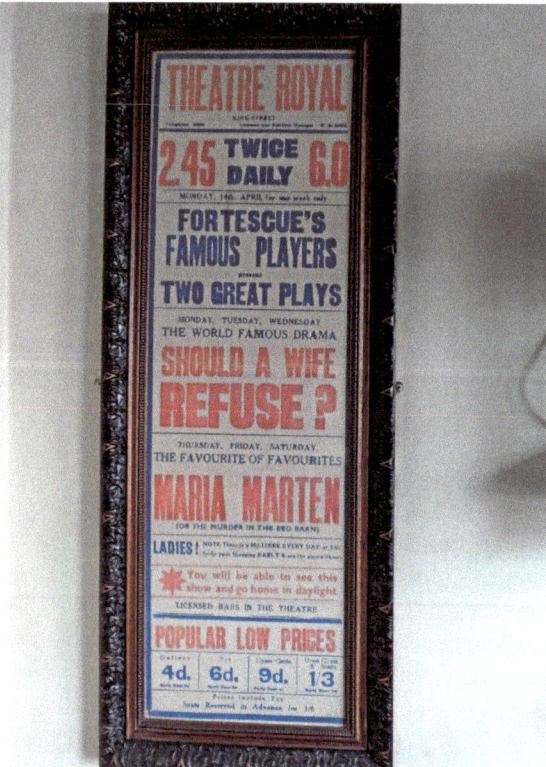

Above: Old figurehead.

Left: Old Theatre Royal playbill.

8. The Old Duke, King Street

Opposite the venerable old Llandoger Trow stands the famous Bristol jazz pub the Old Duke, which although it looks newer is in fact fairly ancient and a Grade II-listed building. In 1775, it was known as the Duke of Cumberland and its landlord, Lewis Jenkins, ran it as an inn that provided board and lodging as well as drink to travellers, the bulk of whom were sailors far from home. In the latter half of the last century, a jazz-loving landlord erected an inn sign bearing a painting of bandleader and maestro pianist Duke Ellington, and the pub entered a new era. The area between it and the Llandoger, which has retained King Street's original cobblestones, was pedestrianised in the 1970s and is now furnished with picnic tables where people can sit and enjoy a drink on warm evenings as they listen to strains of the jazz music that the Duke serves up every night of the year. Once this was mostly of the traditional variety, but nowadays they present a mix that includes blues and modern jazz. I went this week to check it out and was glad I did so because the band on stage, Victoria & the TrueTones, were truly excellent: the musicians polished and professional and Victoria Klewin's voice out of this world.

Life at the old pub has not always been so well ordered. Given its location close to Queen Square, it's not surprising that the Duke was one of many taverns that were attacked during the riot of 1831 by gangs of men demanding drink. In 1862, sailing

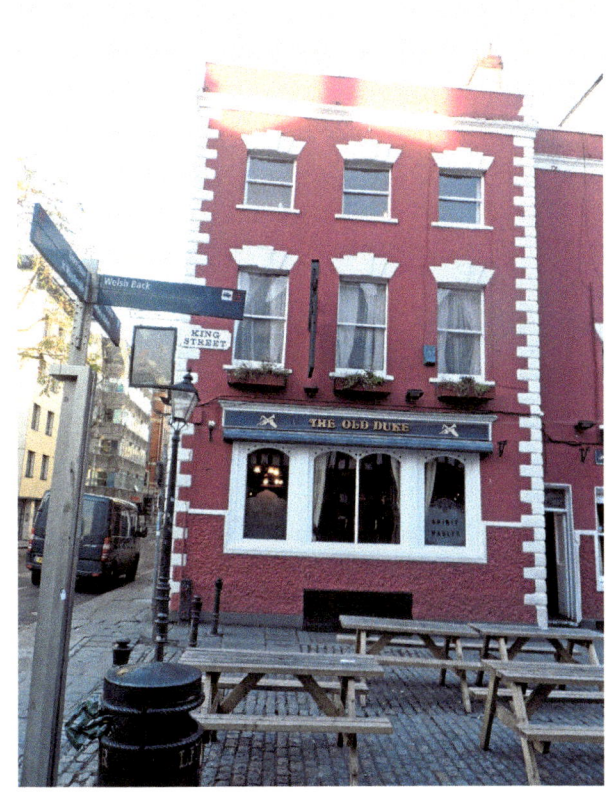

The Old Duke.

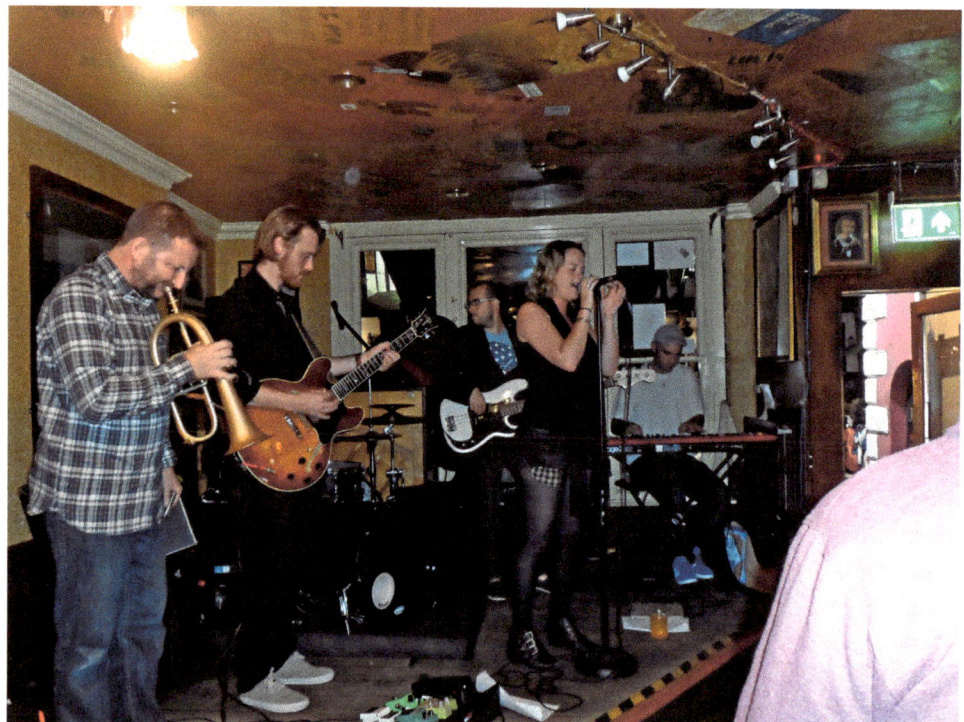

Victoria & the TrueTones.

upriver on the incoming tide was the fastest means of transport into the port of Bristol, and in the summer of that year the pub's landlady, a Mrs Thomas, climbed into a small boat near the mouth of the River Avon to do that. Instead of taking her home as she had hoped it would, though, it capsized almost at once and left her struggling in the water. Fortunately for Mrs Thomas, one of that redoubtable group of men, the Pill watermen, happened to be close by and he flung her a rope. She must have been a good swimmer because she is said to have caught this between her teeth, before grabbing it and being hauled to safety.

9. The Famous Royal Navy Volunteer, King Street

The Famous Royal Navy Volunteer, on the same side of King Street as the Llandoger Trow, at Nos 17–18, is a huge pub made from two buildings knocked into one. How long it has been an inn is a matter of conjecture: there are claims that it was converted to this use in the 1860s when it became the haunt of dock labourers who worked on Welsh Back, but the later date of 1912 has also been mooted. The original houses were part of a row that has been standing since 1665 but there have been many alterations since that time. The original timber frontage was rebuilt in brick in the 1690s and modernised again in 1750, at which time its street aspect was changed again, but some out-of-sight remnants of the original construction remain in the form of roughly chiselled roof timbers secured with wooden pegs. The 'Navy' in the pub's name was recently changed from 'Naval'.

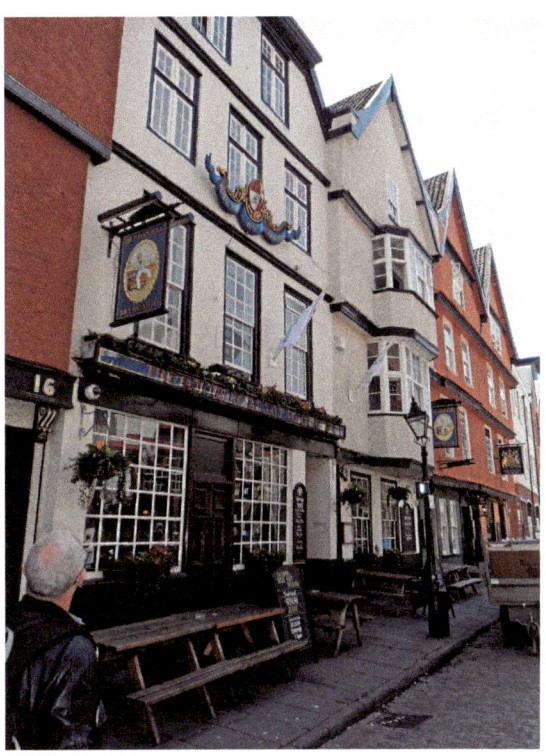

The Famous Royal Navy Volunteer.

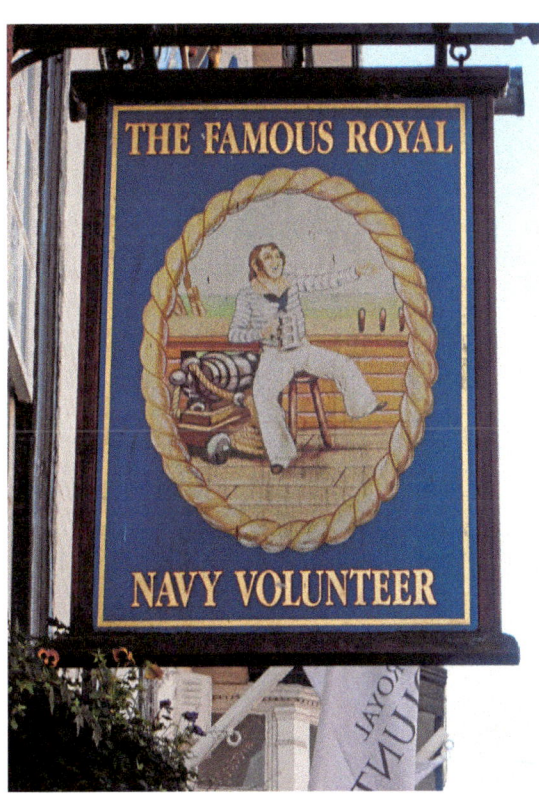

Inn sign at the Volley.

While still a private house, the building was home in 1736 to one of the founders of the Bristol Royal Infirmary, John Elbridge. A member of the Society of Merchant Venturers, he was a collector at the Custom House in Queen Square and in charge of building and allocating quays in the port, but as with many businessmen of the time there was a darker side to his dealings: the source of his wealth was the many slaves he 'owned' on the Spring Plantation in Jamaica.

10. The King William Ale House, King Street

If we like to think of recycling as a twenty-first century invention, we could not be more wrong. One example of how things were reused in bygone days is the pair of cannon, used as bollards, on Welsh Back close to the Llandoger Trow. They were filled with iron to strengthen them for the mooring of heavily laden wooden ships and, strangely, one has a cannonball in its mouth while the other does not. These bollards were not a one-off, there are others outside The Ostrich pub and the old Bristol General Hospital on the harbourside. Similarly, at least some of the wood used in the construction of King Street more than 350 years ago came from ships that had been broken up locally. During a refurbishment of Nos 7–8 in the 1970s, it was discovered that the oak studs

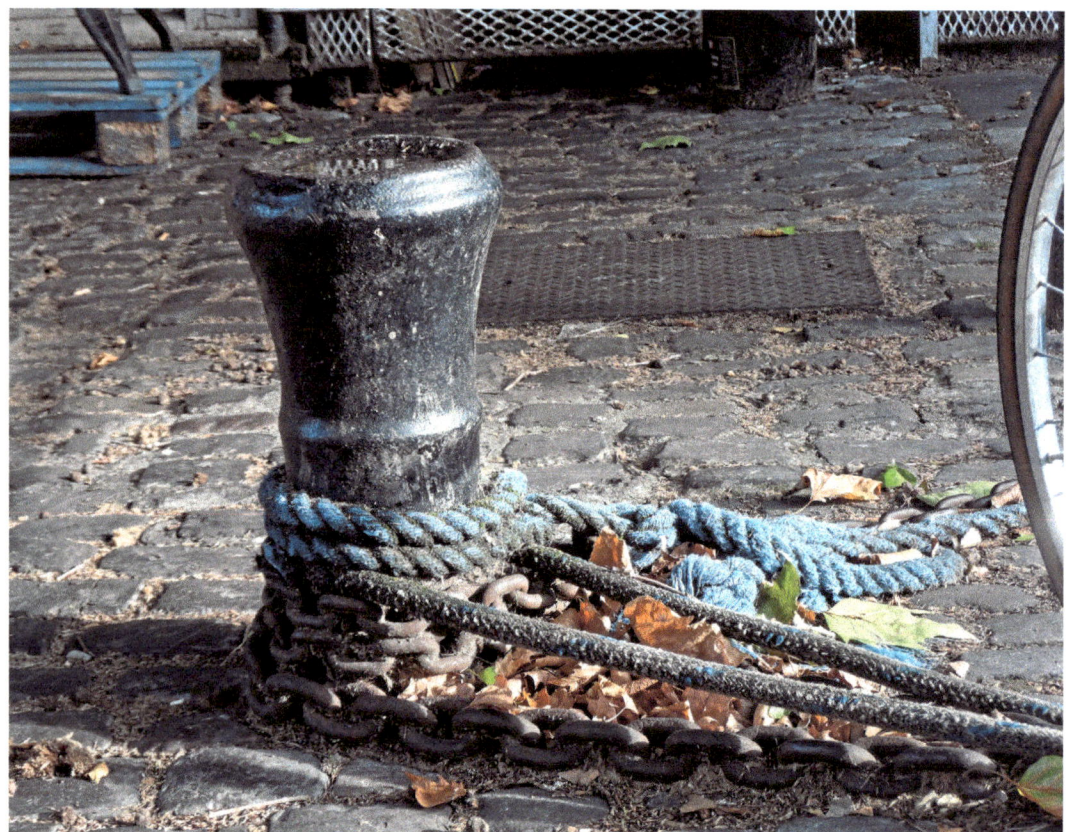

A recycled cannon.

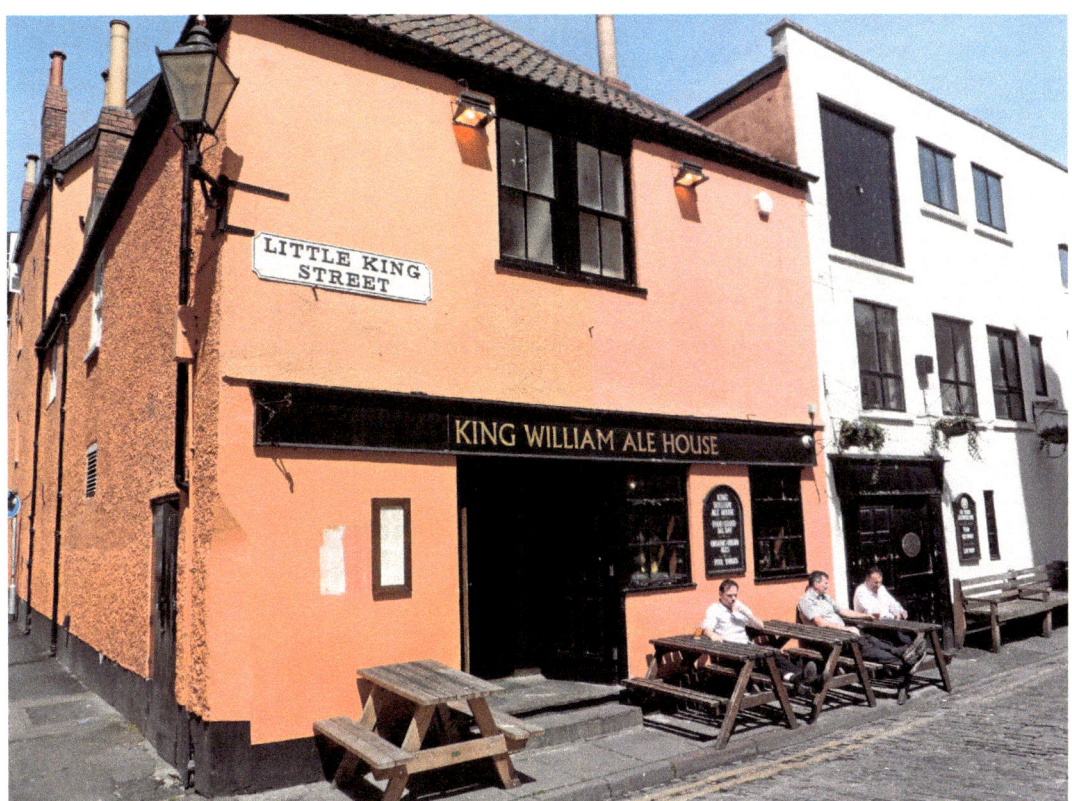

King William Ale House.

and the braces of the building were recycled ships' timbers, and the same is believed to be true of the oak beams that support the ceiling of the King William Ale House.

Built as a refuge for women paupers in 1652, the Grade II-listed building changed its use to a tavern later in the same century. It is a lovely pub, with a blazing log fire in a beautifully carved fireplace during the winter months that provides a warm welcome for its clientele, literally. Unfortunately, at least in your author's opinion, the pub's interior was recently refurbished and the 'snugs', booths big enough to accommodate only four people that once lined the centre, have been taken out. One feature that has remained, which has sadly been lost in all the other nearby pubs, is the rear back block that allows entrance from Little King Street. This was once a common arrangement in old inns, particularly here in the West, and the King William has wisely taken advantage of its rarity by providing picnic tables outside for the patrons, including many local office workers, who prefer to eat and drink *al fresco* on sunny summer afternoons.

11. The Louisiana, Wapping Road

The Louisiana was built in 1809 on the back of Bristol's floating harbour development, the brainchild of water engineer William Jessop, which allowed ships to stay afloat while they were in dock rather than lying beached in the mud as they had done earlier. The pub, originally designed to accommodate seafarers, was first named the Bathhurst Hotel in honour of MP Charles Bathhurst, who must have invested heavily in the development of the nearby Bathurst Basin. At that time, Bedminster was an area of farms and green fields, and to provide its nautical guests with a viewpoint over this bucolic scene, the architect had a local smith design and build a balcony on two of the pub's sides. It was canopied to keep them dry on rainy days, and together with the rounded shape of the Louisiana's southern wall, must have made the beached sailors feel as if they were standing in the bows of a ship. The pub catered for seamen right up until the 1960s, since which time it has had several different incarnations. For many years it was also known as the Bathurst Tavern, and in 1978 it was renamed the Garrick when the licensee of a long-gone inn that stood nearby, the Garrick's Head, took it over and wanted to retain his old customers. The pub was renamed the Smugglers in 1982 but its resemblance to the kind of building seen on Bourbon Street in New Orleans makes its present name, the Louisiana, suit it best.

During the massive Bristol Riot of 1831, the governor of the nearby New Gaol on Cumberland Road, William Humphries, was taking refreshment at the inn and watched helplessly as rioters wrecked his institution, freed the prisoners, set fire to the gallows and the huge, twenty-man treadmill, dragged them out and flung them

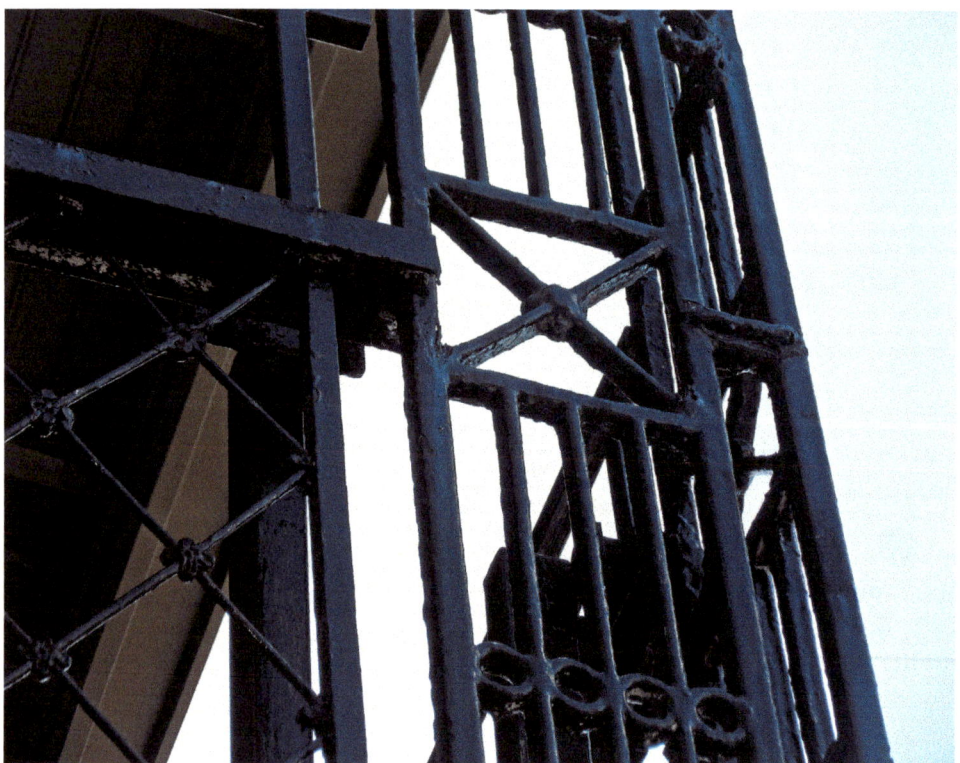

Ironwork on the Louisiana's balcony.

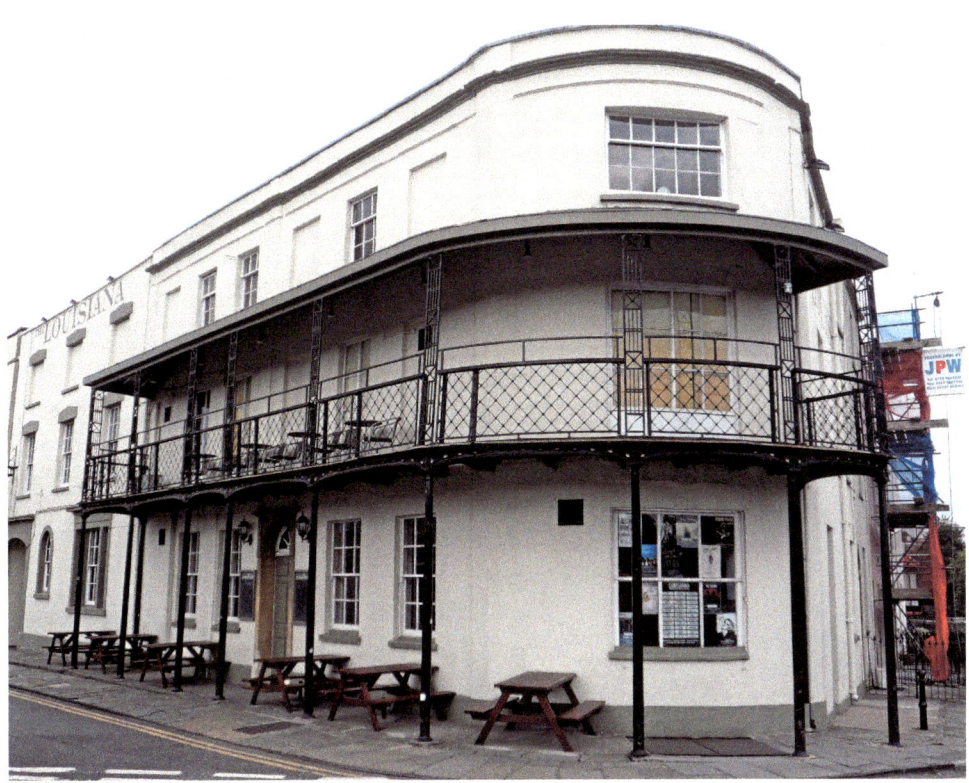

The Louisiana.

into the river. Only the prison gateway was left intact. This had a trapdoor in it so that public hangings could take place, and it was put to use afterwards when four rioters who were seen as ringleaders were executed there. Bristol's last public execution was in April 1849 when Sarah Thomas, eighteen, who had beaten her elderly employer to death with a stone before killing her mistress's dog and stuffing it down a lavatory, was hung there.

The Louisiana's inn sign is pleasantly weathered and the metal fanlight above the entrance door, a smaller version of the one at No. 10 Downing Street, is in a style much favoured in Bristol when the inn was built. The architect's ideas may have been a little too grandiose for the inn's owners, since many of its window were later bricked up, doubtless as a result of the iniquitous window tax introduced by William III in 1696. This taxed buildings on the number of windows they had, and was wittily dubbed 'daylight robbery'. The tax remained in force for over 150 years before being scrapped in 1851, condemned by campaigners as 'a tax on health, light and air.'

Opposite the Louisiana, on the edge of the New Cut, which diverted the tidal River Avon as part of Jessop's reorganisation of Bristol's inner waterways, it is easy to miss the small strip of land known as God's Garden. This provides a pleasant walk only yards from the noise and fumes of the city.

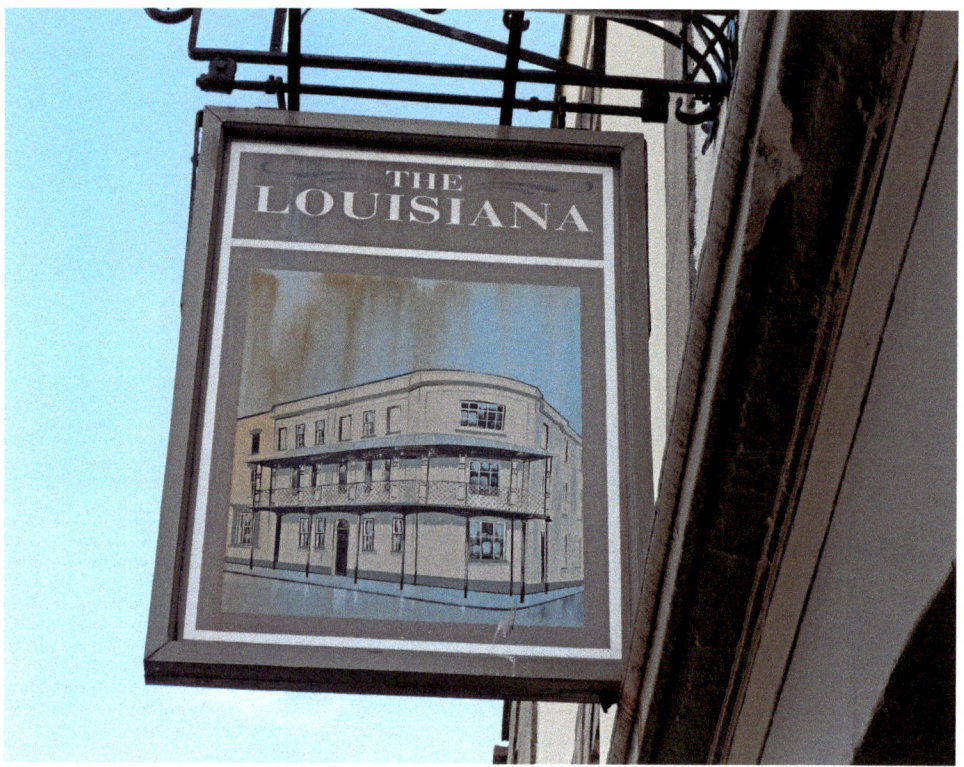

Louisiana pub sign.

12. The Ostrich, Lower Guinea Street

The first record of a victualler holding The Ostrich Inn is that of Jonathan Marn in 1775, but it seems certain that this Georgian quayside pub is somewhat older, with 1745 being the most likely date of its construction. Originally, seafarers and dockers were its main clientele along with shipyard workers, since ships were built nearby from ancient times; John Cabot's caravel the *Matthew*, which sailed from Bristol to Newfoundland in 1497, may have been built at Redcliffe as was its replica almost 500 years later. During The Ostrich's early days both the Bathhurst Basin, on which it now stands, and the adjacent New Cut along which the River Avon was diverted, lay far in the future. The inn was actually built on the bank of the Avon close to Treen Mills, where the clear waters of the River Malago were discharged into a millpond said to have been known locally as the Oyster Reach, which may mean that the inn's name was a corruption of those words. This is not as improbable as you might first think, though, as there were two other pubs called The Ostrich in late eighteenth-century Bristol, one in Old Market and the other on Durdham Down. When Charles Bathurst MP provided the finance to redevelop the area as part of water engineer William Jessop's design for the floating harbour in 1809, he modestly renamed the inn the Bathurst Hotel, a name that probably died when he did.

The Ostrich continued life as a working man's pub, with rail workers added to its clientele around 1897 when the Bristol Harbour Railway smashed its way through

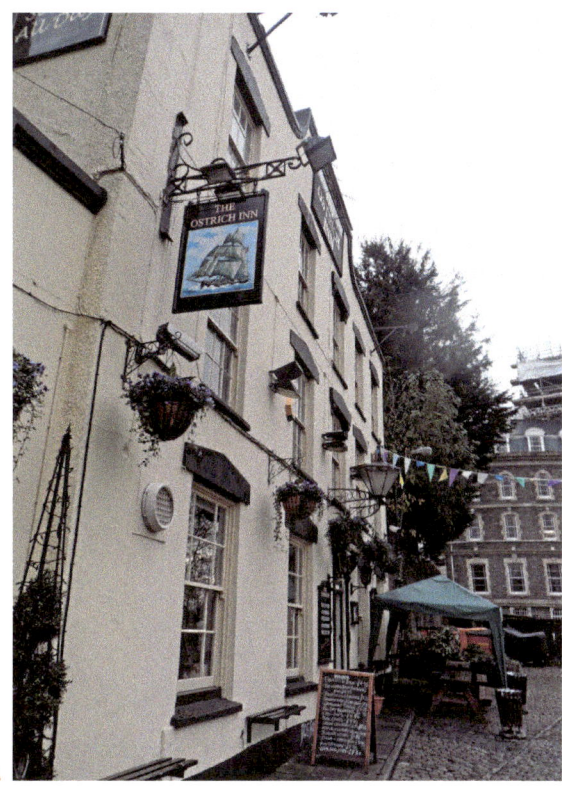

Right: The Ostrich Inn.

Below: The cave in The Ostrich bar.

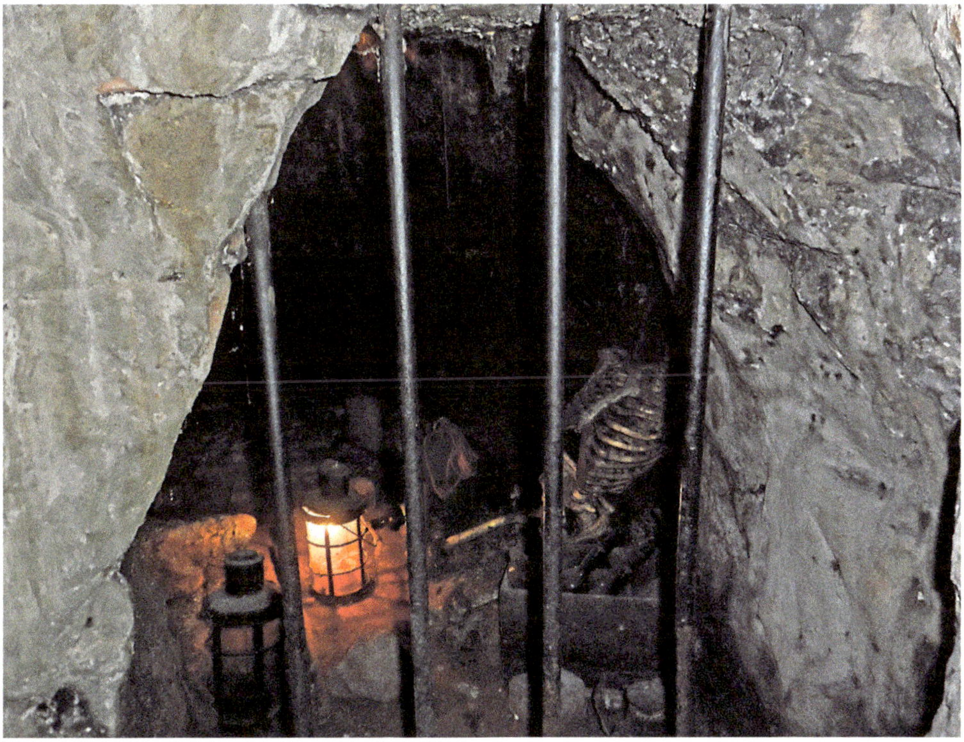

Redcliffe Caves to cross the Basin on a steam-powered bascule bridge, roughly where the blue-painted footbridge stands today. The bricked-up exit of the rail tunnel can still be seen to the right of The Ostrich. The rail link closed in 1964, and a decade later commercial sea traffic in the area was officially pronounced dead. The Ostrich deteriorated to a rowdy, semi-derelict scrumpy house but when the area was redeveloped, with bijou harbour residences and berths for houseboats and leisure craft, its waterside location gave it a new lease of life.

Today, the pub makes much of its nautical past with what's inside. There is actually a cave in its bar, a tiny part of the extensive Redcliffe Caves complex that was probably nothing more romantic in the past than a storeroom. The management has wisely placed some dusty wine bottles and a replica skeleton inside to fuel the myths about pirates and smugglers that surround the pub to this day.

13. The Golden Guinea, Guinea Street

A stone's throw from The Ostrich stands the Golden Guinea, extravagantly claimed to be 'Bristol's best back-street boozer' by its present owners. The building certainly dates from the early 1700s, although the exact date is not known; it probably started life as a private house and later became a shop. Both the pub and the street on which it stands are named after Guinea in West Africa, which later became known as the Gold Coast.

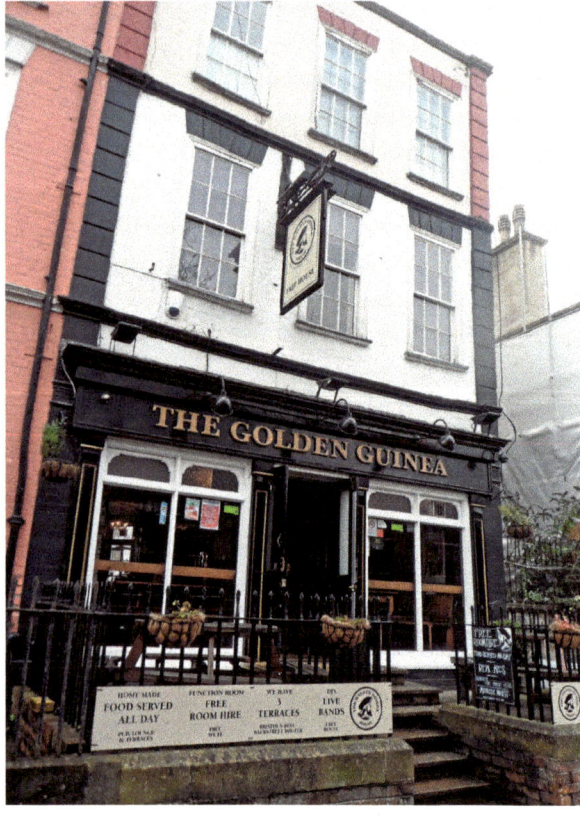

The Golden Guinea.

Some early examples of the golden coin with which the pub and the street also share their name bear the Elephant & Castle symbol, badge of the Royal African Co., which had a monopoly on the slave trade until 1698, when Bristol gleefully joined in the shameful commerce. Given the nature of the triangular trade, in which kidnapped human beings were exchanged in America for tobacco and sugar, it is significant that in 1797 a refinery or 'sugar house' was erected at the harbour end of Guinea Street.

Surprising, the Golden Guinea had no direct link with slavery. Up until 1975 it was actually called the Victoria, a name that must have gone back to at least the middle of that queen's reign since 1861 it was listed as a 'beer shop and eating house.' Guinea Street was once home to slave captains like Edmund Saunders, who commanded twenty slaving expeditions yet held the post of Warden at nearby St Mary Redcliffe, and Joseph Holbrook who offered a reward to anyone catching his runaway slave, 'Thomas, a native of the island of Jamaica, who speaks good English and wears a brown wig.' Much of the original street has been lost to redevelopment. Some buildings were destroyed when the Bristol General Hospital was built in 1831, and many that stood opposite were demolished in the 1870s when Bristol Harbour Railway smashed its way from Temple Meads to the docks. At that time there were many pubs with a nautical flavour in the street including the Jolly Sailor, the Two Anchors and the Sailor's Return.

Nowadays, the Golden Guinea is a lively place with events almost every night: music, quizzes, comedy, open mic and more. The candles in Chianti bottles are a tad clichéd for your author's taste but the leather sofas are comfortable and, like the Real Ales, the ambience is good.

14. The Seven Stars, Thomas Lane

If you enjoy pubs with comfortable armchairs and gourmet food, give the Seven Stars a miss. On the other hand, if you like an authentic inn that has been in the business for centuries and sells a constantly changing range of Real Ales, then this is the place for you. The pavement outside still has iron-bound edges to prevent damage by the metal rims of cartwheels; these were unique to Bristol and you may still spot them in other places in the city. Inside, the bare wooden floor and oak beams couple with an array of posters and pictures to make this backstreet pub a real gem of the rough diamond variety. It's not stuck in the past, though, there is a jukebox and a pool table as well as Grolsch and Amstel on tap, and if you are interested in one of the more esoteric ales on sale the barman may let you sample a mouthful before you buy, and you cannot get fairer than that.

The Seven Stars claims to date from the 1600s but was probably purpose-built in the following century. Whichever version of history you choose, when you look at a building that old it is easy to think, 'I'll bet that place has some stories to tell'. In fact this little, out-of-the-way pub in an easily overlooked lane in Bristol has a past that sets it on the stage of world events. In 1787, a red-haired man, taller than most at the time, turned up there and formed a rapport with its landlord, Mr Thompson. The new arrival was Thomas Clarkson, the intrepid campaigner whose lifelong work in exposing the shocking reality of slavery was to provide the facts that William Wilberforce would later use in Parliament to bring about its abolition. Slavery was

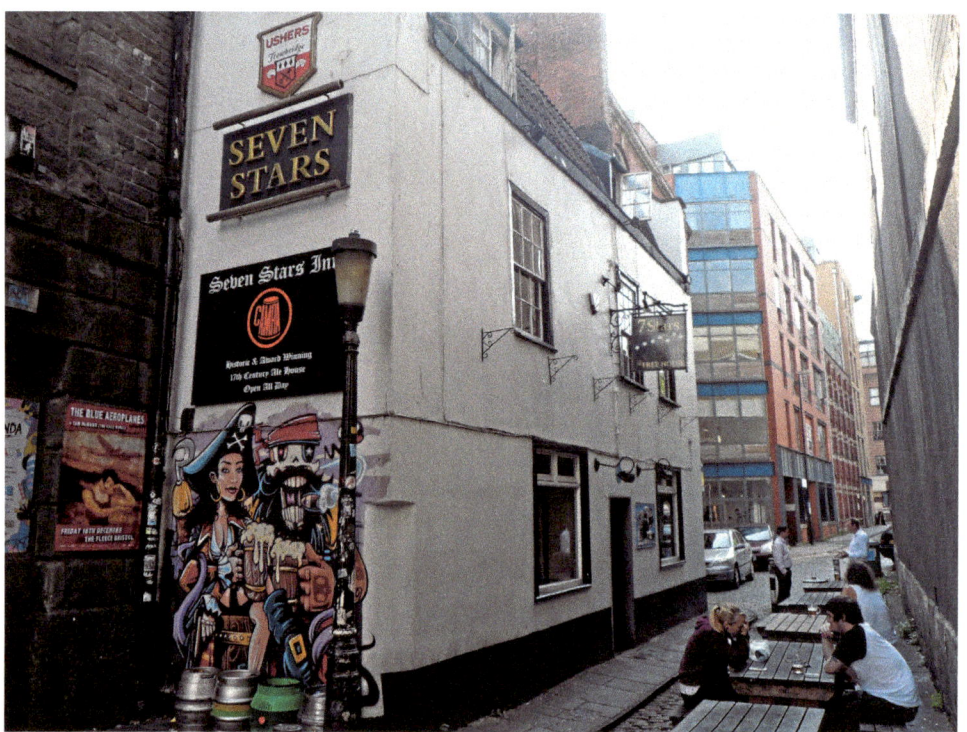

Above: The Seven Stars.

Below: Plaque outside the Seven Stars.

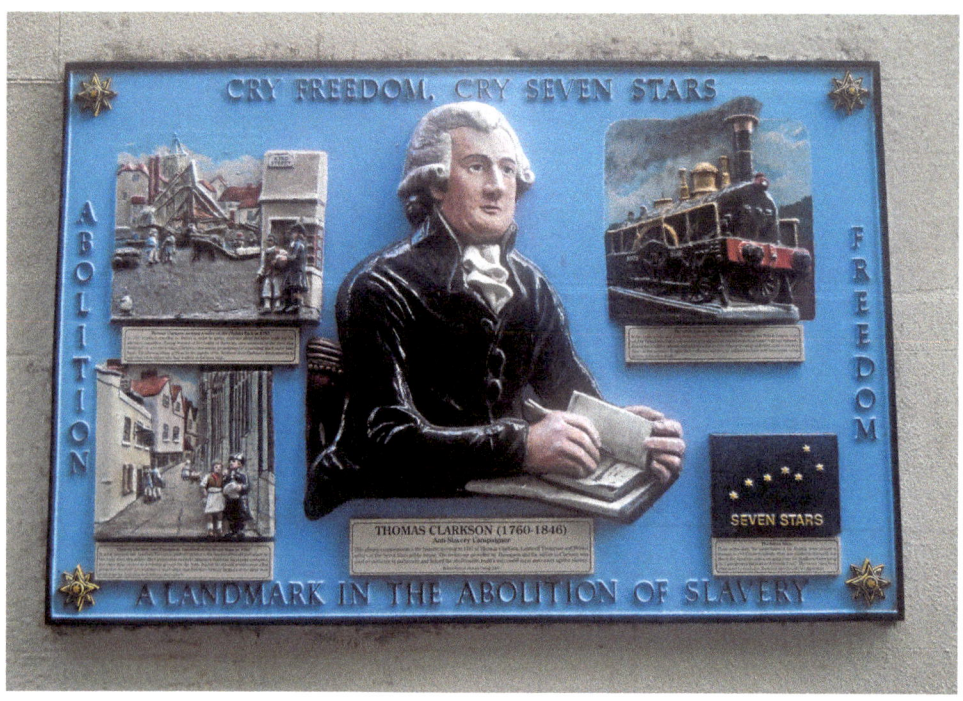

the mainstay of Bristol's economy and the impetus for its growth, and Clarkson had arrived in the city with some trepidation, he is even reputed to have blackened his hands and face like a miner so that he could blend in with its working men. In Mr Thompson he found a kindred spirit, and together they saw to it that the truth about slavery came out, including its heavy death toll among the sailors who were often conned into the working on the slave ships or sometimes simply kidnapped like the slaves themselves.

On the wall outside the Seven Stars there is a plaque, erected by Bristol Radical History Group, whose colourful images portray the pub's role in these momentous events.

15. The White Hart, Maudlin Street

A White Hart in chains and wearing a golden crown was the heraldic badge of Richard II, who ascended to the throne in 1377 at the age of ten and remained king until he was deposed and imprisoned four months before his death in 1399. That is almost three centuries before the date of 1672 proudly proclaimed on the pub's front wall as the date of its construction, and it is highly likely that the name was carried over from an older inn that once stood on the same spot. Indeed, there is evidence that the hostelry began life as the Chapel of St James Priory – Bristol's oldest building – which stands behind it. Founded by Robert of Gloucester

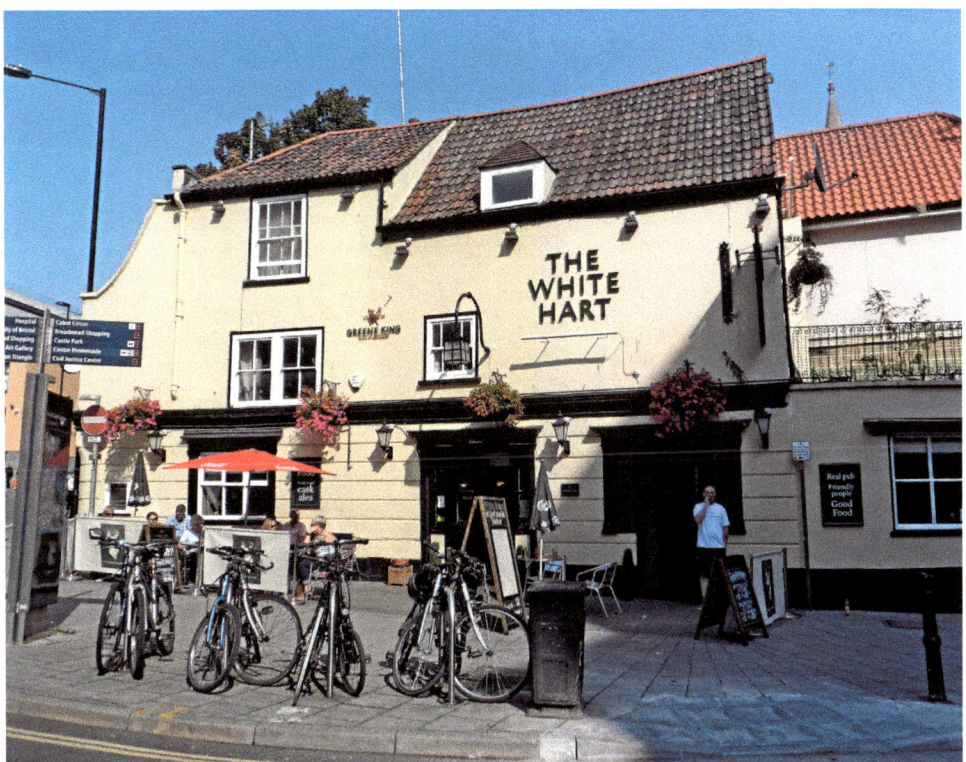

The White Hart.

in 1129, the priory is a building that should not be missed by anyone with even a mild interest in the city's history. The Benedictine order of monks, who occupied it then and still do today, have a reputation for hospitality. As commonly happened in those far-off times, they gave the chapel over to accommodating pilgrims and others who found themselves shut out from the old walled city when nearby St John's Gate was locked at night.

The low doorway that leads into the White Hart attests to its age, as do the beams that support its ceiling. Situated beside the bus station and close to the Bristol Royal Infirmary, it will always be assured of regular custom from these sources but is also popular with a wide cross section of Bristolians.

From 1857 until 1880 the White Hart's landlord was one Daniel Thatcher. Five years into his tenure he employed a woman called Elizabeth Tiggle who arrived without a reference, proved unsatisfactory and was sacked. Later Mrs Thatcher spotted Elizabeth in the street wearing clothes she had stolen from the inn and had her brought before the Police Court, where she was sentenced to two months' hard labour.

16. The Drawbridge, St Augustine's Parade

This old pub in the heart of the city centre has always been a favourite for evening revellers and the fact that it is right next door to the Bristol Hippodrome, as well as many offices and shops, ensures that it attracts customers every day of the week.

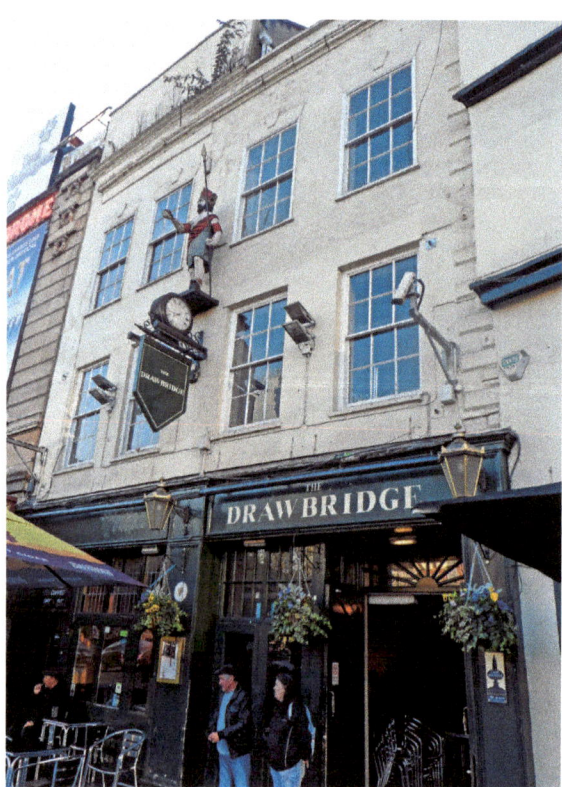

The Drawbridge.

The River Frome, which ran outside its front door until the council had it covered over in 1893, was crossed by means of a drawbridge, which gave the pub its name. In 1990 the pub's owners, for reasons known only to themselves, renamed it the Horn & Trumpet, which Bristolians, always ready to lampoon pretentiousness, immediately christened the Horny Strumpet.

The Drawbridge has some interesting tales to tell. The carving over the clock on its façade was the sculptor's idea of what a Native American would look like, and wears a headdress made of tobacco leaves. This provides a tenuous link to Bristol's past as it is a copy of the figurehead of a Victorian paddle steamer, the *Demerara*, which ran aground in the River Avon in 1851. Demerara was the old name for Guyana, scene of a violent slave revolt in 1823. The figurehead, transferred to a building, which was demolished in 1930, was copied for the Drawbridge.

One early morning in January 1920, the pub's licensee, Mrs Brown, was woken by police hammering on the door. She flung a coat over her nightie and fled in a shower of broken glass from the fanlight as flames from a tyre store behind the pub licked the rear of the building. She gained sanctuary in the nearby Bristol Tramway office and watched as her livelihood was saved.

17. The Christmas Steps

Christmas Steps is one of the relatively few remnants of old Bristol to survive the Second World War. A plaque at the top of Christmas Steps proclaims, 'This Streete was steppered Done and Finished September 1669.' At the bottom of the Steps, facing the medieval fish and chip shop, there is a public house that has catered for drinkers for the past 300 years. Until recently it was called the Three Sugar Loaves, a name that connected it to those mainstays of the economy in eighteenth-century Bristol – the slave trade and sugar. Perhaps because the pub is largely out of sight, its present owners have chosen to cast aside centuries of history by naming it after the historic Steps on which it stands. In the 1700s, sugar refineries moulded their raw material into cones, which, because of the great heat of the process, were handled with tongs. The pub's delightful old inn sign showed these elements and we can only hope that it has been kept, in case the name is ever reinstated. The pub was actually named after a nearby refinery that burned down – one of eleven to do so between 1670 and 1859. Only one remains today, the former Sugar House, now the Hotel du Vin, nearby on Lewins Mead. There were once at least five pubs bearing the name Sugar Loaf in Bristol but today only one remains, on St Mark's Road in Easton.

Insurance premiums for sugar houses were frighteningly expensive and as a result, local businesses devised their own insurance schemes and employed local fire fighters. This was fortunate for the Three Sugar Loaves when it caught fire one hot August night in 1847, posing a threat to a neighbourhood described at the time as 'thickly populated.' Despite the arrival of several firemen with a fire engine, by the early hours of the morning the interior was almost gutted, while flour in Merry's bakery next door was also destroyed by fire. Fortunately the pub's landlord, Thomas Richards, was insured and received £300 with which to rebuild.

On two levels, the Christmas Steps serves English and continental foods as well as Real Ales, and has events most nights to attract customers to its tucked away location.

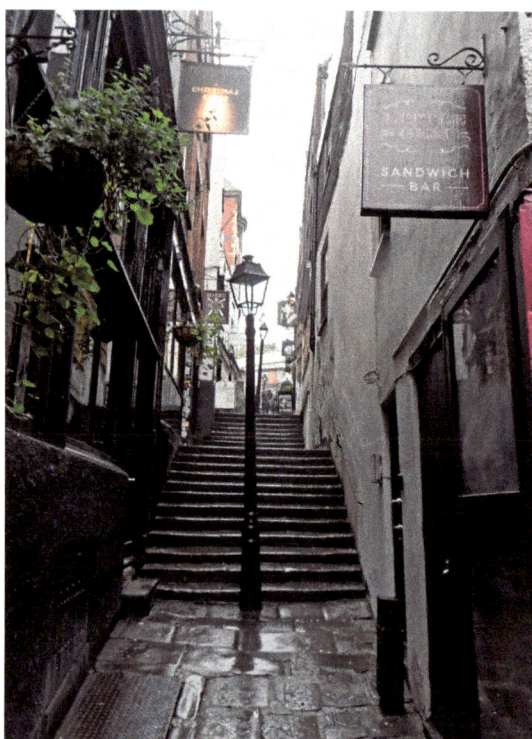

The Christmas Steps.

18. The Shakespeare Tavern, Prince Street

This old pub, a Grade II-listed Georgian building, adopted its name to capitalise on its closeness to the Theatre Royal in nearby King Street. It was designed in 1725 by John Strachan as one of a terrace of fine townhouses, of which only three remain, built for Henry Combe and John Becher. Both men were slave traders, plantation owners and merchants, and the houses they built were joined to their warehouses, which backed onto the Narrow Quay. At the death of a friend who had owned a sugar plantation in Jamaica, John Becher's wife Mary received an unusual bequest of 'property', which she described as, 'my negro boy named Tallow'.

When it was around fifty years old, probably in 1777, the house was converted to an inn, and its current claim to be 'the longest serving ale house in Bristol' may be true, but do not let the Hatchet in Frogmore Street hear you saying so! The Shakespeare's first recorded landlord was John Farrall. In its early days it was the haunt mainly of dockers and warehousemen, but this was not always the case. In 1783, the landlord was a freemason called John Hopkins, who ensured that it was patronised exclusively by rich merchants, ship's officers and captains, so that 'few mariners below the rank of boatswain' dared to enter it. In 1806, the pub was known briefly as the Shakespeare & American Tavern.

Inside, the first thing you will see is the Shakespeare's wonderfully crafted, curving mahogany staircase that faces the entrance. Sadly, there is little else of antiquity to be seen within this very fine pub, whose closeness to Bristol's waterside, theatres and club land will assure it of a future at least as long as its past.

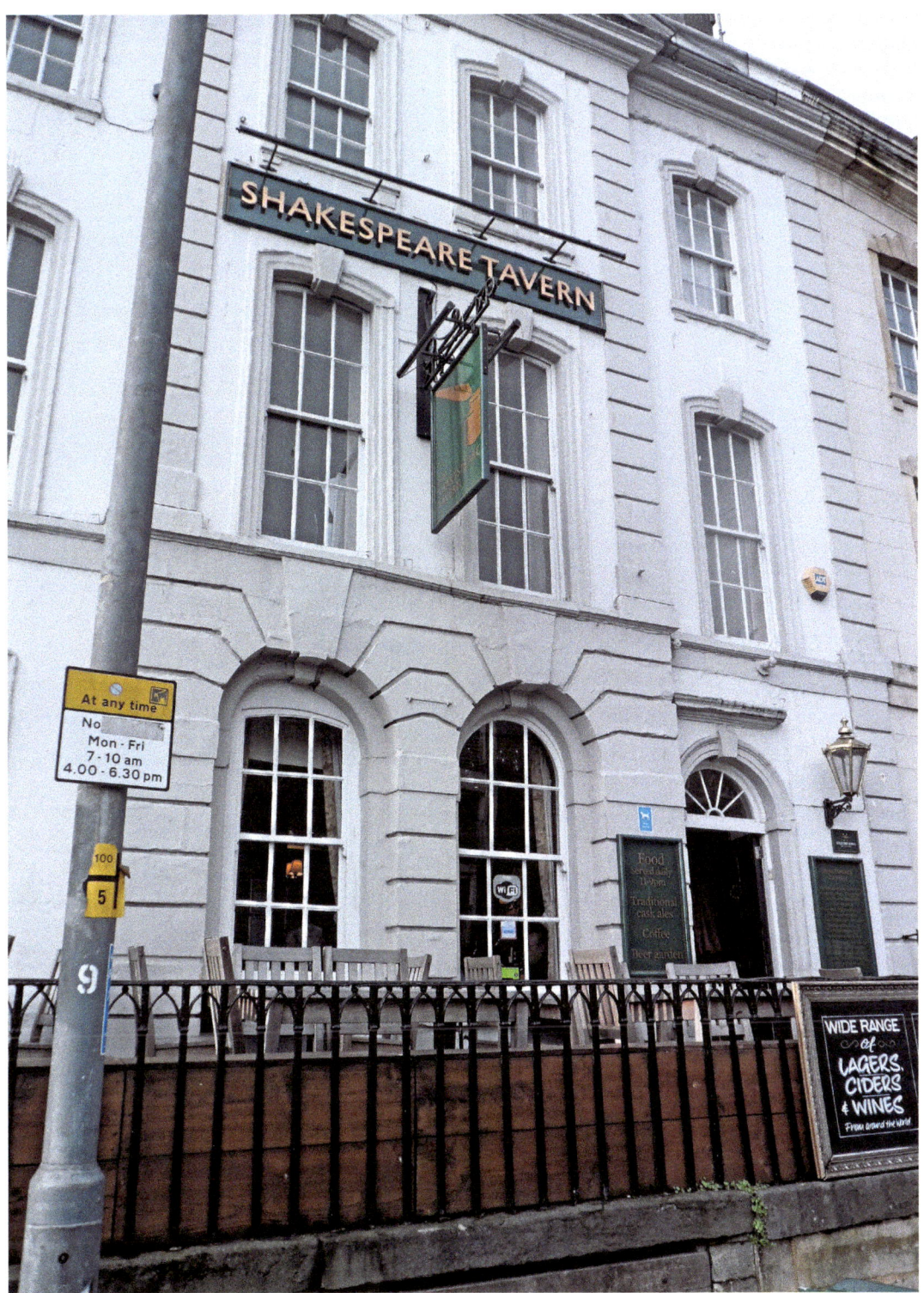

The Shakespeare Tavern.

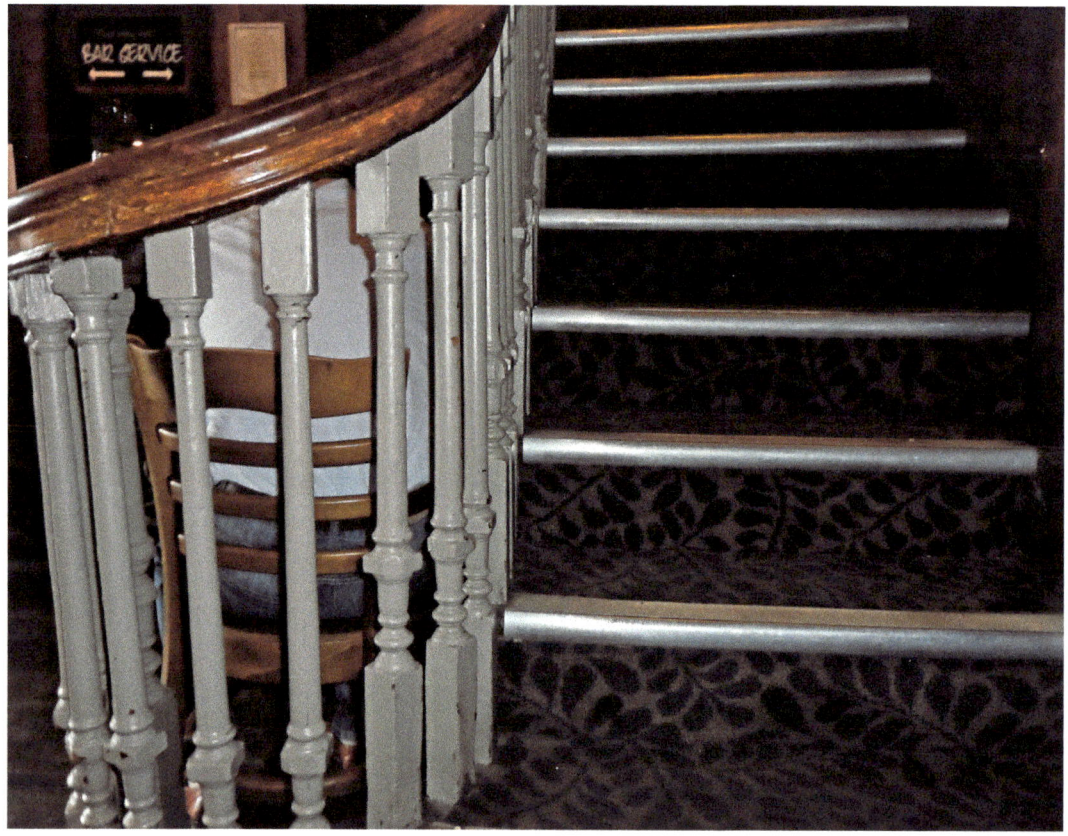

Staircase at the Shakespeare.

19. The Boardroom, St Nicholas Street

This fine old tavern is a gastropub these days and caters for the more discerning palate among the office workers who throng its interior during the day, and the upmarket drinkers who patronise it during the evenings. Although it is more interested in cheeses than cries of 'Cheers!' these days, it has a long history as a drinking establishment named the Elephant – a heavy clue to this waves its trunk at you from the front wall. There has been an Elephant pub at this spot since the 1600s, and in 1853 the present pub was known by the quaint but unwieldy name of the Elephant Wine & Spirit Vaults & Slate Billiard Rooms. In late 1857, the landlord, John Vowles, was assaulted by a woman called Bridget Ryan when he tried to eject her for drunkenly annoying his other customers. Bridget bit him on the arm and ripped his clothing before being taken to the Police Court where she was fined 1s 6d – 7 and a half pence in today's money – with the alternative of seven days in prison.

In around 1863, the original pub was knocked down as St Nicholas Street was redesigned and broadened by Henry Masters, the Victorian architect who added the stone elephant sculpture to the building's front before it reopened in 1867. The Elephant must have continued to function somehow during the upheaval, perhaps

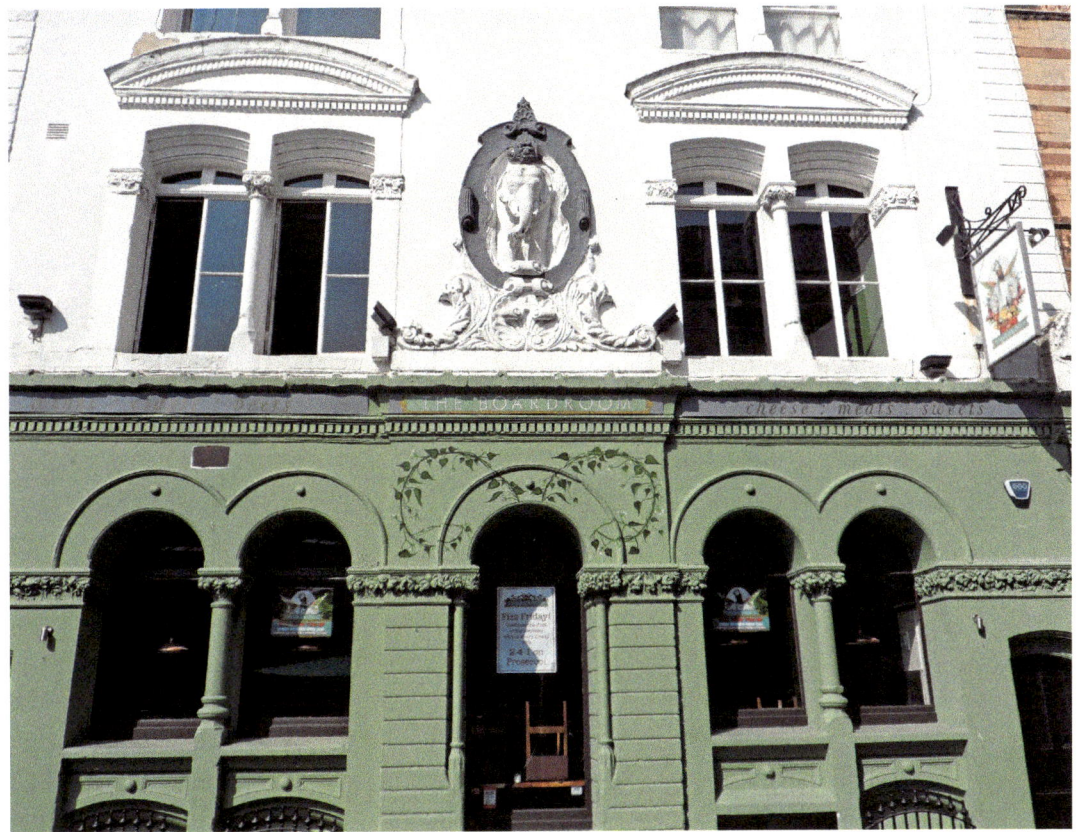

The Boardroom.

at the premises nearby, since John Vowles remained as landlord, announcing his retirement in 1881 but apparently carrying on until 1883. The pub changed hands then but not for long: in 1885 John's daughter Alice took it over.

In more recent times, the Elephant was for many years Bristol's most famous – some would say notorious – gay bar. Incredible as it may seem today, during the 1970s the U-shaped bar had a glass partition at one end with men staying to the left and women to the right. Eventually the partition was removed, yet this voluntary apartheid continued long afterwards. I am told that there used to be a poster in the pub depicting two elephants, one sniffing the other's bottom with the caption, 'Don't Leave Your Friends Behind'. The present bar/restaurant must have foreseen a struggle with this colourful past when it decided upon its present image, hence the change of name and the toning down of the once brightly coloured animal that adorns its front wall.

Nowadays the gay scene has moved to the Pink Village around Old Market, where coincidence has it that another pub designed by Henry Masters, the extraordinary Palace Hotel, is a focal point.

2

North

20. The Colston Arms, St Michael's Hill

Edward Colston (1636–1721) was described by Bristol Corporation, then an alliance of rich entrepreneurs, as 'a person ever memorable for his benefactions and charities' and 'an example of Christian liberality'. While it is true that he founded Colston's Hospital School and donated huge sums of money to setting up almshouses and maintaining

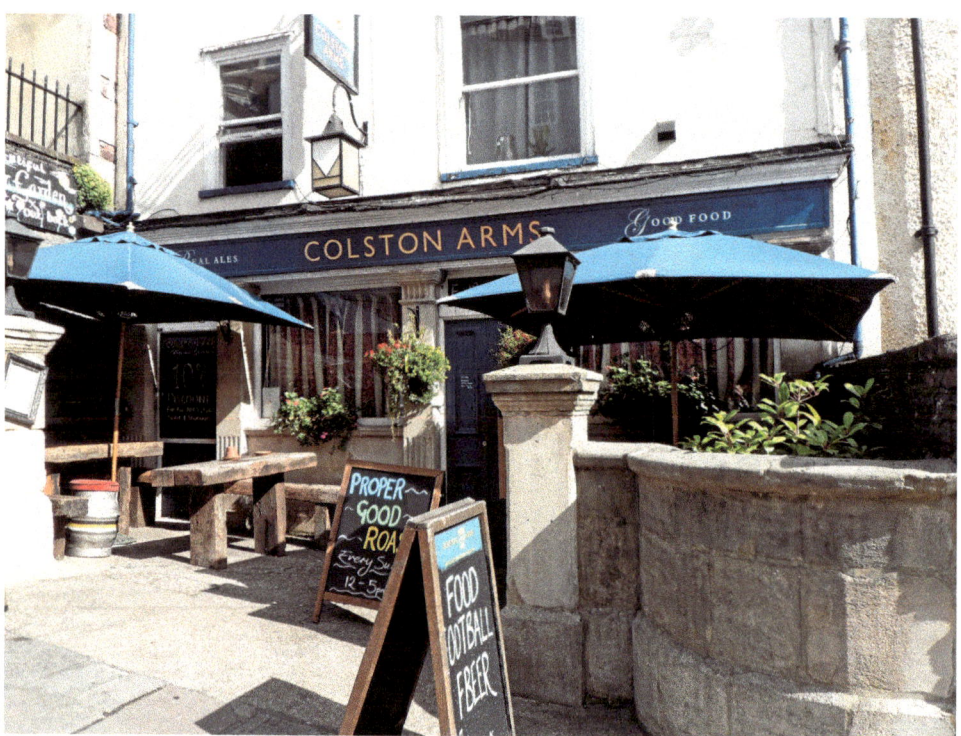

The Colston Arms.

vicarages, contemporary commentators apparently found it easy to ignore the fact that his wealth was derived from the slave trade, whose hundred years of brutality had to wait almost two centuries to be surpassed in horror, and only then by the Holocaust.

The pub looks deceptively small from outside but the interior is spacious with a comfy snug, a small bar in front and one at the rear leading into a beer garden. Exactly how old it is was difficult to establish. For one thing, in the directories of 1863 and 1879, its address is listed as No. 59 St Michael's Hill whereas today it is at No. 24. The Grade I-listed Colston's Almshouses next door were completed in 1696 and the Arms, which is definitely Georgian, may have been built in the late 1700s. Edward Roche ran the pub in 1816 and when John Cochrane, landlord from 1829 until 1848, died after a painful illness, his wife Ann took it over. Fanny Davis was granted the licence in 1914 and had the pub until the eve of the Second World War. In more recent times, the boozer was run by a Welsh rugby fanatic who may also have had a penchant for Charles Dickens' *David Copperfield* as he renamed the place Micawbers. The pub sign carries Colston's coat of arms featuring waves, an anchor and a pair of dolphins.

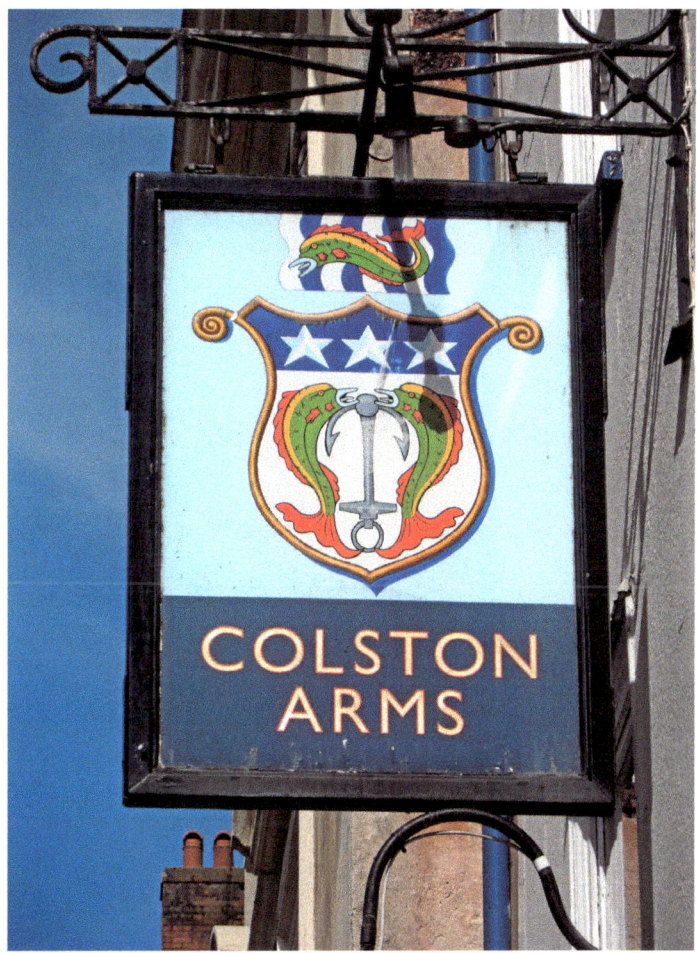

Colston's coat of arms.

Nowadays the live sport TV is popular with the area's many students, who also enjoy live music there from time to time. Other locals like the fact that dogs are allowed inside and there's not only a quiz night but also a Cinema Club. Real Ales compete with standard beers and cider at the bar, and if the food is marginally more costly than other nearby establishments, this is reflected in its quality and a range that includes traditional Sunday roasts, Ploughman's with West Country cheddar, rare breed pulled pork and oak-smoked Scottish salmon.

21. The White Bear, High Kingsdown

On the far side of the street at the very peak of St Michael's Hill stands one of the oldest pubs in Bristol, the White Bear. There has been an inn at this spot for centuries for the simple reason that it once stood on what used to be the main road to Wales. It offered a resting place for horses that had just made the tortuous climb up the hill, which is steep even by the standards of Bristol, which, like ancient Rome, was built on seven hills. Formerly a house called the Green Dragon, it was known as the Swan in 1752 when John Bevan was landlord, and may have been rebuilt in 1760 when it was given its present name, perhaps by William Bower who was landlord in 1764. William's wife or daughter, Sarah, took over the following year. The pub was extensively refurbished again during the nineteenth century but still has what was once its stable entrance.

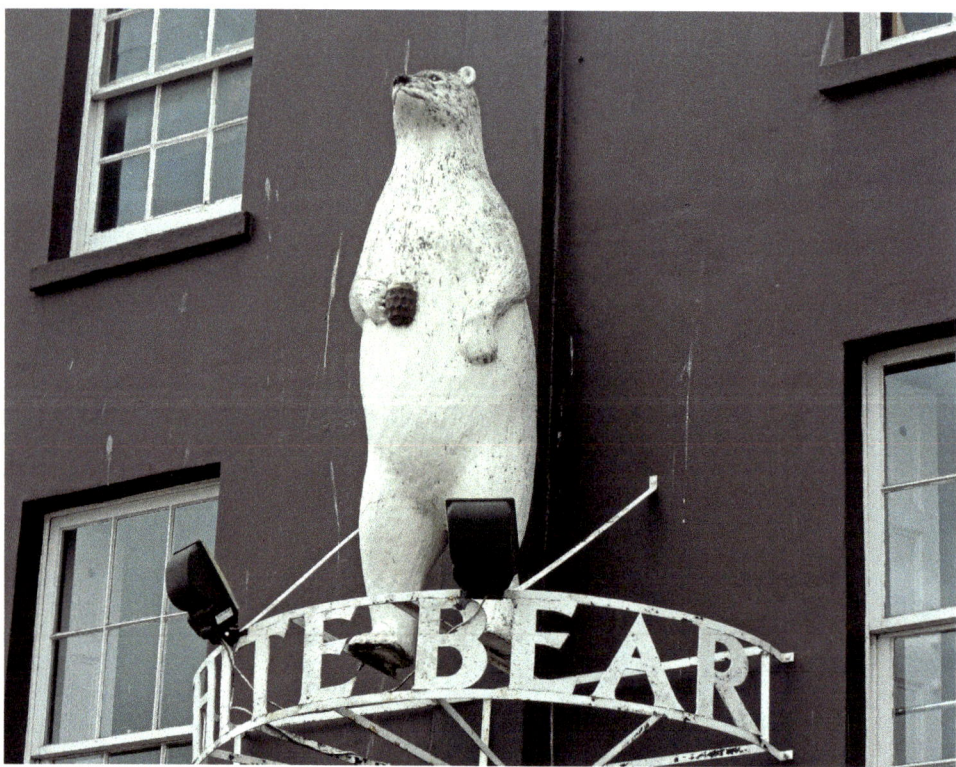

Pussycat White Bear.

Today it is a lively place whose clientele are mostly young and often drawn from the student population at the nearby University of Bristol. It serves food in the afternoons and evenings including vegetarian dishes, and there is a big-screen sports TV in the patio garden at the rear where the brewhouse once stood. The pub hosts quizzes, barbecues and film nights, and talks and shows are held in a room upstairs. All excellent events, but I cannot help wondering if the artist who sculpted the model of a white bear outside the pub had a grievance against the management, and wanted revenge. Readers may agree that the animal looks just like a pussycat.

22. The Highbury Vaults, High Kingsdown

Public executions were a favourite spectacle in old Bristol as in other cities, and for centuries before the opening of the New Gaol on Cumberland Road the favourite spot for holding them was Gallows Acre at the top of St Michael's Hill, roughly where the Cotham Road roundabout stands today. In 1555, seven Protestant martyrs were burned at the stake there on the orders of Queen Mary, and in 1781 Ben Loveday and John Burke were convicted of buggery and sentenced to hang there in what was probably the last death sentence for the 'crime' of homosexuality to be carried out in Bristol. Executions continued until the early 1800s but, though it is difficult to

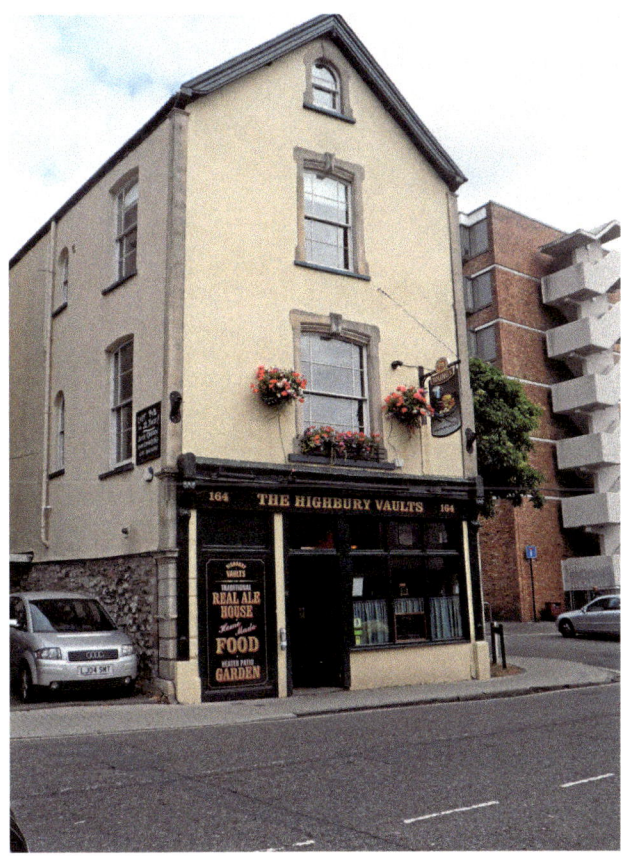

The Highbury Vaults.

ascertain with any certainty just when the Highbury Vaults was built, it seems certain that it was the last stop for felons on their way to the gibbet. The story is that they had a last bite to eat and a tankard of ale before going to their deaths.

In 1871, when William Partt was landlord, the pub was known as the Highbury Wine Vaults, and the inside can have changed little since. There is a small snug at the front for those who wish for privacy, and the way the long interior is panelled in dark wood gives the place a special atmosphere. The rear patio garden, once a venue for the so-called sport of cockfighting, is now a pleasant spot for a drink on a sunny afternoon, and set into a wall there is another relic of our barbaric past, displayed as a curiosity: the old inn sign showing a condemned prisoner, which your author remembers hanging outside as late as 1980. Another feature worth noting is the graffito of Rapunzel on the outer wall. Its creator, Nick Walker, is said to have influenced the early Banksy but if that is true then they have now undergone a role reversal, since the painting owes a lot to Banksy's cheeky comment on marital infidelity at the bottom of Park Street.

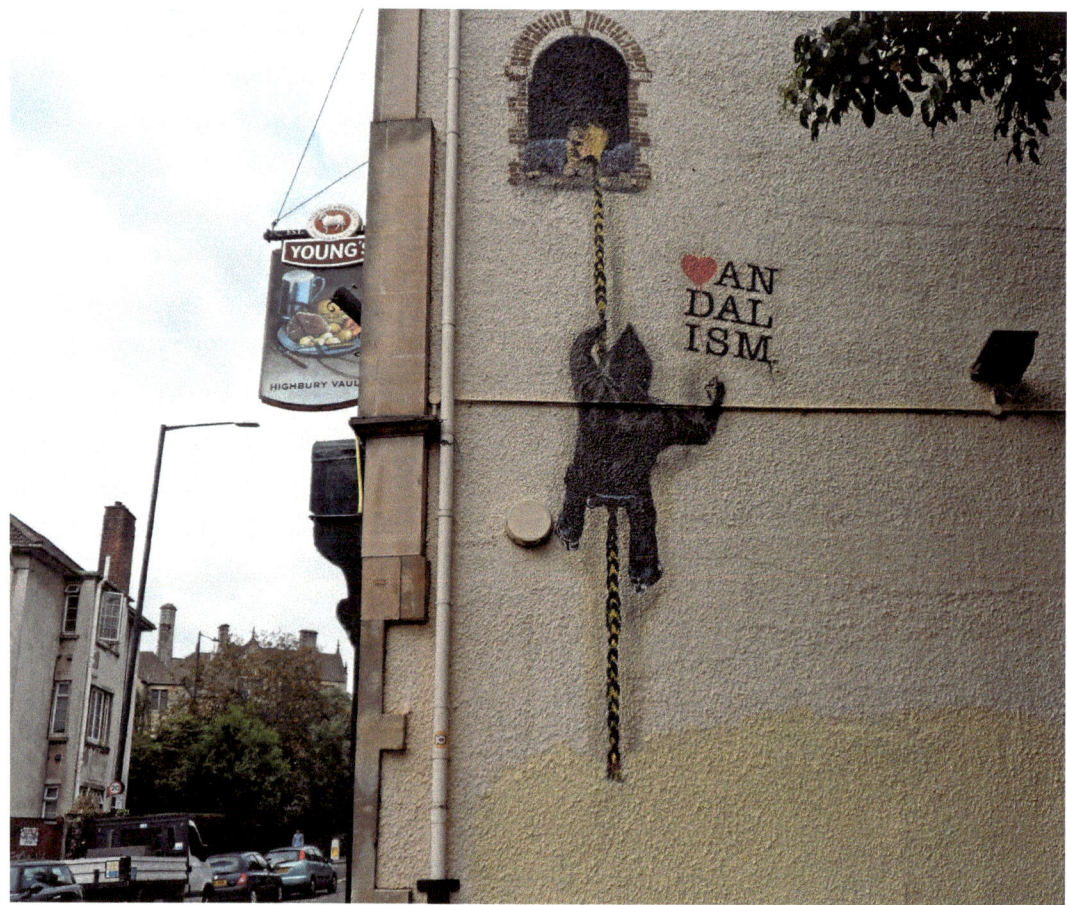

Highbury's Rapunzel.

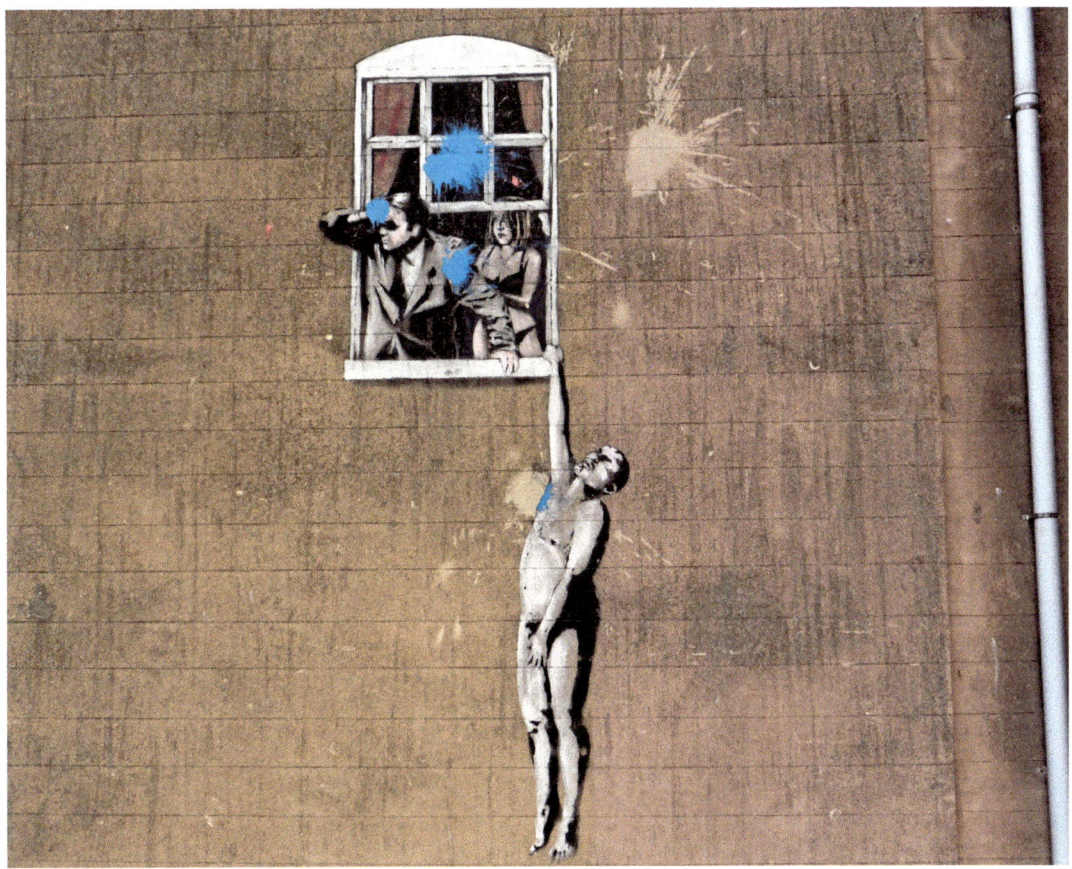

Banksy from Park Street.

23. The Cotham Porter Stores, Kingsdown

Even though they lived in an era when many people could not read and write, when there was none of the competition boozers face today from forms of entertainment like radio, TV, cinema and the Internet, not to mention supermarkets selling cheap beer, the Victorians knew how to build great pubs. The Cotham Porter Stores is a case in point. The first licensee recorded was R. L. Bodley in 1840. The pub was called the 'Stores' as it is today, which was still the case in 1852 when George King gave up his occupation as a draper to run it, but sometime after 1857 it became known as the Cotham Porter House. This was certainly still its name at the outbreak of the First World War in 1914, and the pub kept it until the 1930s when it became known once more as the 'Stores'.

When the Beatles played the Bristol Hippodrome in November 1964 they had to be smuggled into the building disguised as policemen because of the crowds of screaming girls outside, and an enduring story connects them to the Cotham Porter Stores. Legend has it that after the show the Fab Four braved the climb up St Michael's to enjoy a lock-in at the pub during the course of which John Lennon, pleasantly mellow on rough cider, was given black paint and a brush and drew the sketch of a rural drinking

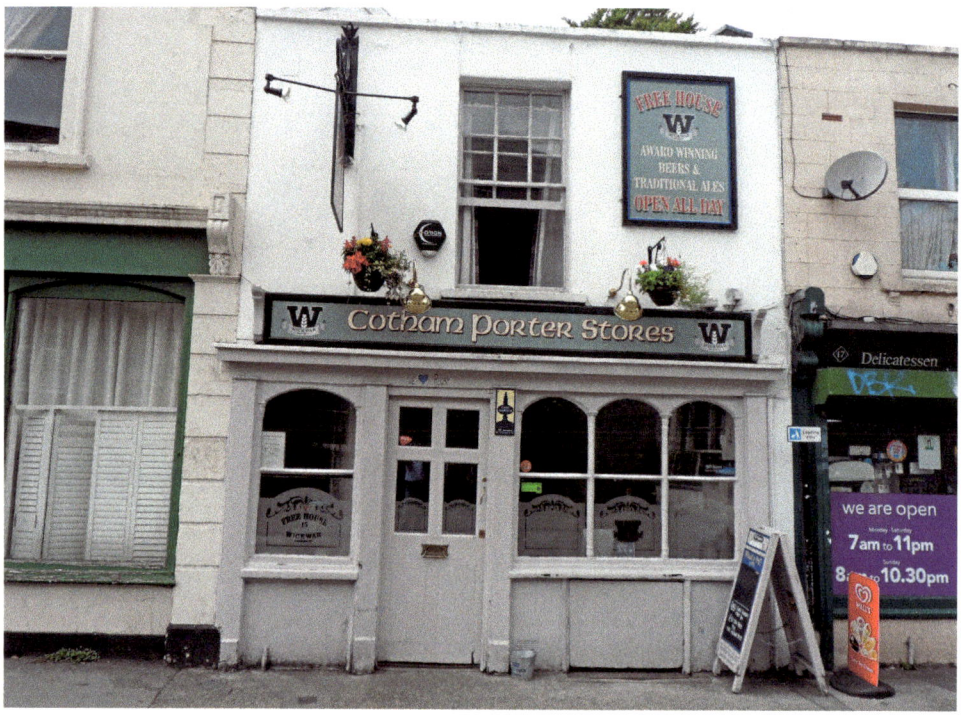

Above: Cotham Porter Stores.

Below: Porter Stores' inn sign.

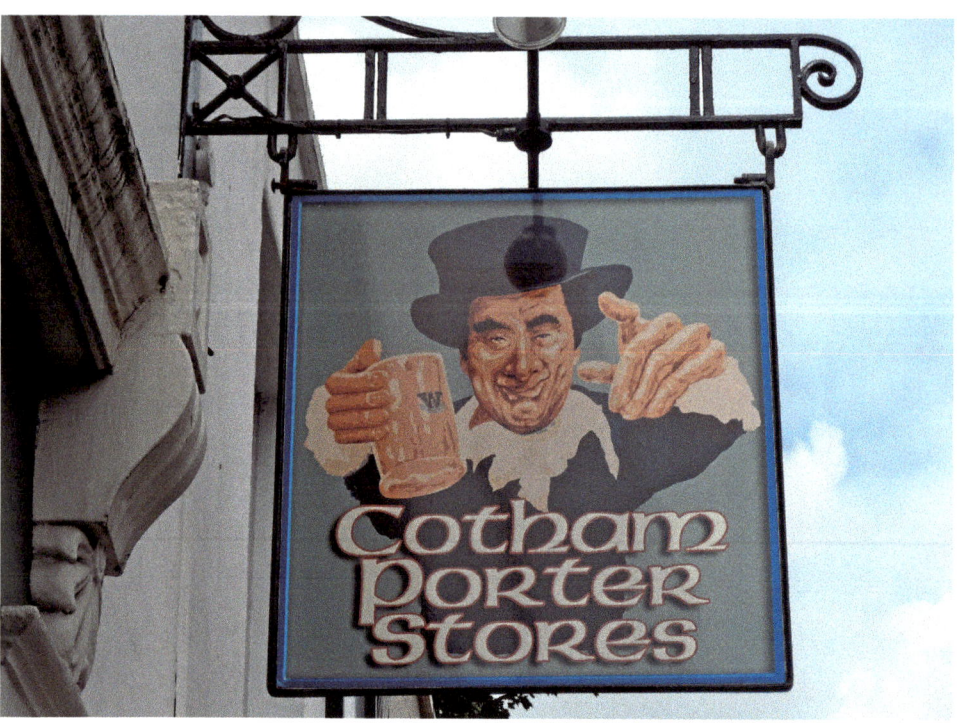

scene that you still pass today as you head for the toilets out in the yard. It's a good story, if hard to substantiate, and all I can say about its authenticity is that it certainly resonates Lennon's distinctive style. Unfortunately, its dark situation and the reflective varnish made it impossible to photograph so the reader will have to have a look for themselves.

The Stores is a true local but don't let that put you off as strange faces are always welcome. When your author washed up in Bristol in 1976 the pub almost exclusively sold rough cider that needed a slice of lemon to add a tang of sharpness to its taste. It still does today but when it was taken over by the South Gloucestershire brewery Wickwar, it added its present array of Real Ales. There's a good natured quiz night on Thursdays and the current landlord's enthusiasm for Rugby is reflected in posters on the walls. What's to dislike?

24. Cat & Wheel, Cheltenham Road

At the bottom of Cotham Brow, at the boundary between Cheltenham Road and Gloucester Road, stands the Cat & Wheel, built in the same era as the unmissable Victorian railway arch in whose shadow it stands. In 1895 the landlord was Tom Asby. The pub's name is actually a corruption of the words 'Catharine Wheel', which has nothing to do with the like-named firework but refers to the death of St Catharine of Alexandria, a Christian martyr said to have been put to death on a spiked wheel. An inn

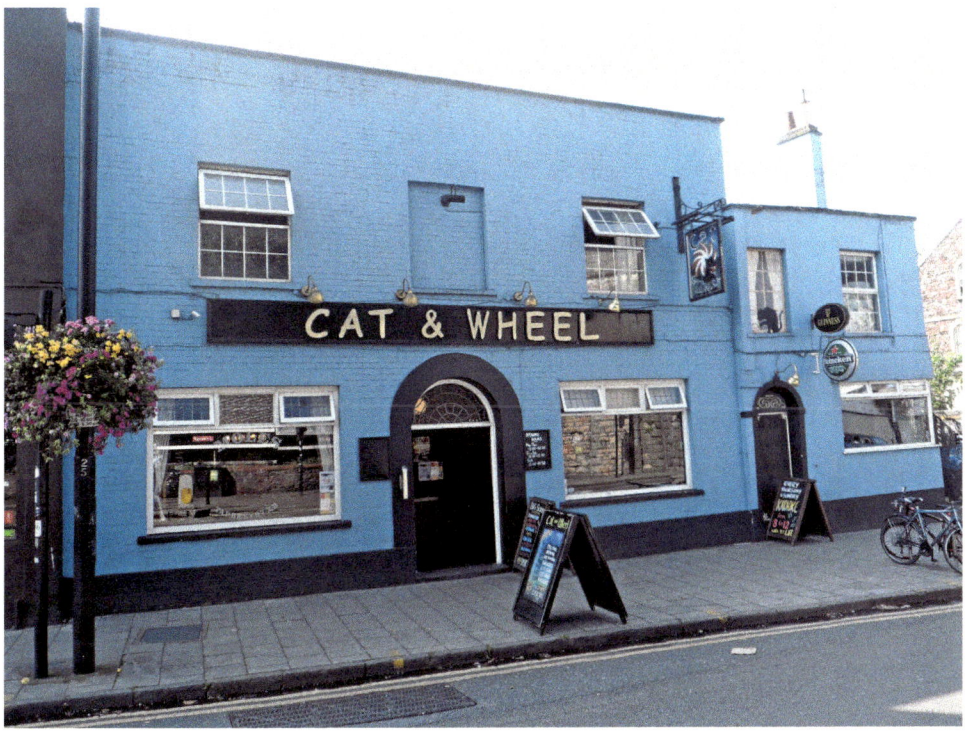

The Cat & Wheel.

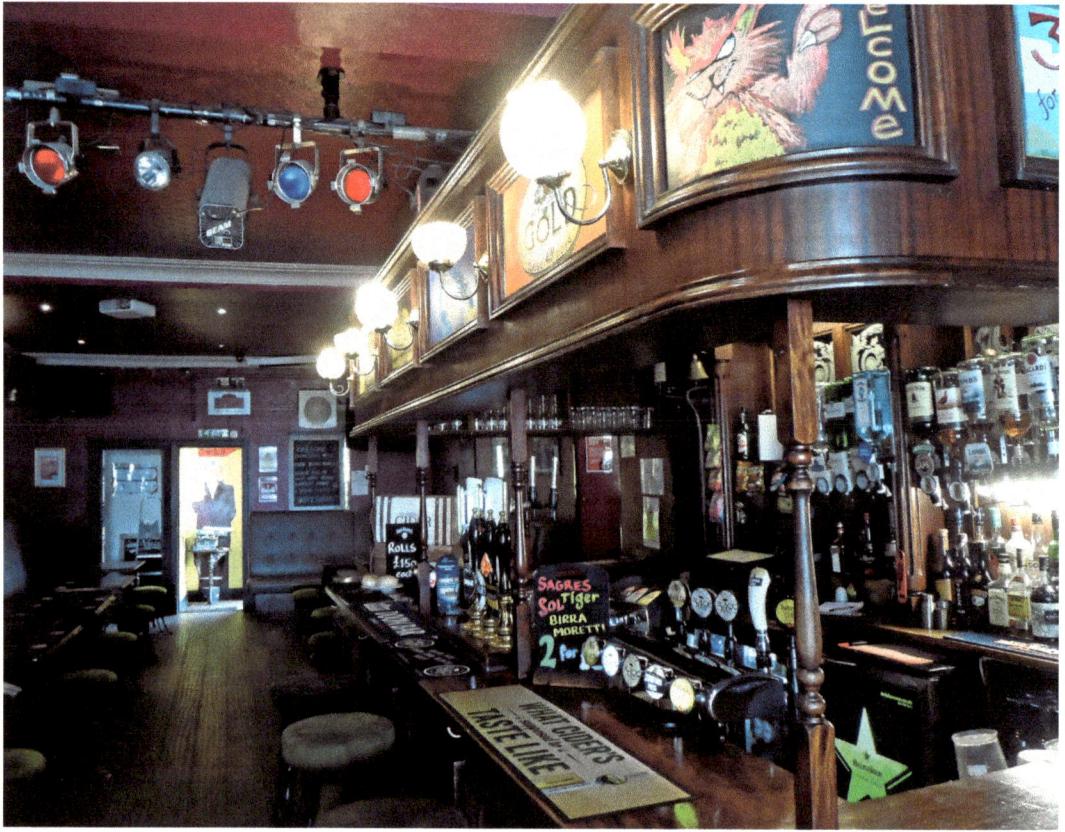

Cat & Wheel lounge.

with the same name stood for many centuries in Castle Street and even survived the Blitz, only to be demolished in the 1960s to make way for the Broadmead shopping centre; an earlier Cat & Wheel may have stood on the same spot as today's blue-painted pub. One school of thought maintains that the change of name happened in the English Civil War when Bristol, a Royalist stronghold, was occupied by Parliamentary Puritan soldiers, the Roundheads. The story is that, because Catharine's Wheel referred to a Catholic saint, letters in the inn sign were painted over to leave 'Cat in Wheel'.

Today's Cat & Wheel, owned by Moles Brewery of Melksham, claims to have Bristol's longest running quiz night. It spotlights live bands on Fridays and Saturdays, provides karaoke, pool and darts and has five widescreen TVs showing sport beneath its high ceilings and heated beer gardens. Not surprisingly, most of its customers are young and there is a fair smattering of university students among them.

25. The Old England, Montpelier

In 1747, the word 'croft' referred to a field, and it must have been pleasant to walk over the meadow of Stokes Croft, through the turnpike to Montpelier. Originally named the Old English Tavern, the inn was not built as a single entity but as part of

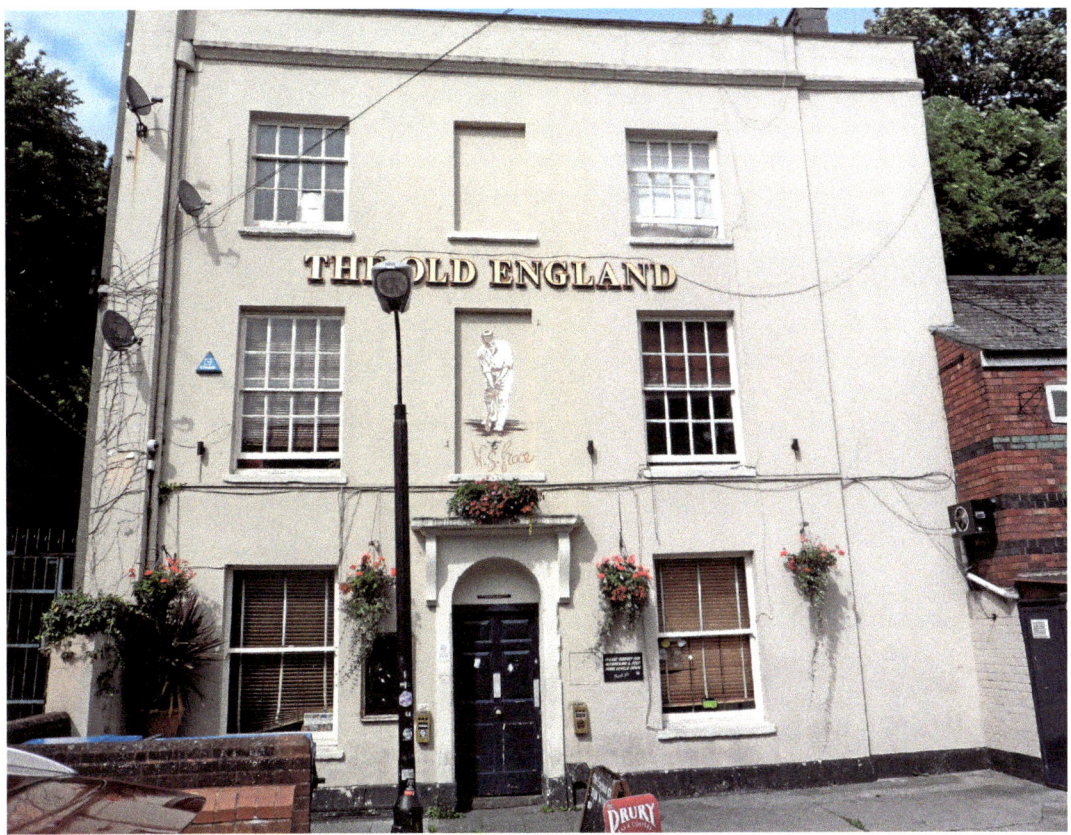

The Old England.

what we would now call an entertainment complex. A snuff mill powered by Cutler's Mill Brook had previously occupied the site and when its millpond began to be used by swimmers, a manufacturer of cotton threads, Thomas Rennison, saw a money-making opportunity and rented the land. His venture must have been successful because in 1764 he bought the place, added a coffee house and a ladies' pool, and advertised his rural attraction as 'Rennison's Grand Pleasure Bath & Gardens'. Next came a bowling green, a tea garden and the pub we know today, whose outward appearance has changed little. The open-air terrace is still a pleasant place to enjoy a drink on a sunny afternoon, and with the little park next door it is all that remains of the spot where the cricketer W. G. Grace once delighted spectators with his skills.

Nearby is Picton Street. It is, without doubt, the best preserved Georgian shopping street in England, a fact that the city council have yet to capitalise upon. Archie Leach, who made his name in Hollywood as Cary Grant, had his boyhood home there for a while. Montpelier is home to many Bristolians of Caribbean ancestry and the street's name is ironic since it recalls General Picton, a governor of Trinidad renowned for his cruelty to slaves. The General was responsible for 'pictoning', an agonising torture where the victim was tightly trussed and suspended with all his or her weight on one big toe,

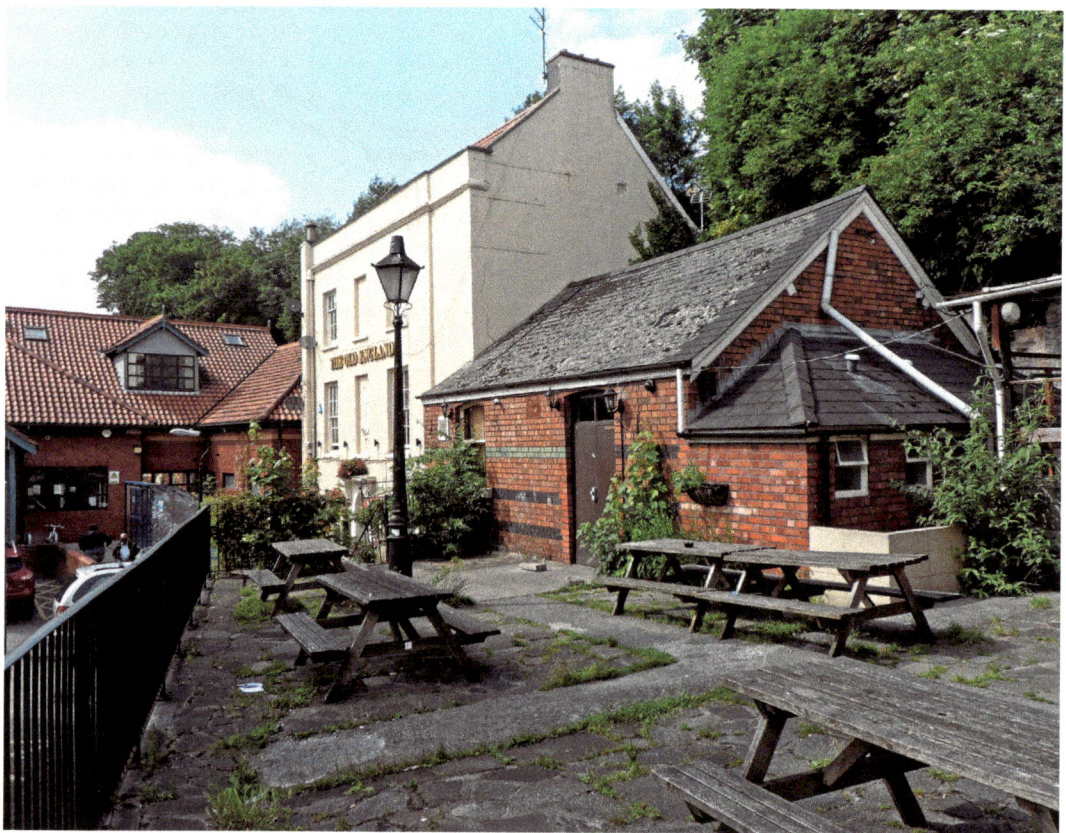

Old England terrace.

which was placed on a pointed stick fixed to the floor. Eventually, General Picton went too far, and after sentencing slaves to death without trial and pictoning a thirteen-year-old free mixed-race girl, Louisa Calderon, he was brought to London to face trial. This fizzled out without coming to a conclusion. He was killed at the Battle of Waterloo.

When the turnpike was demolished to make way for Tuckett's Buildings at the corner of Ashley Road in the late Victorian era, skeletons were found in the ruins, reminders of the time when criminals were hung at turnpikes or suicides were buried at crossroads. Which of these was the case with these sad piles of bones, no one knows.

3

South

26. The Cornubia, Temple Street

On the night of 24 November 1940, hundreds were killed or injured in Bristol when the German Luftwaffe carpet-bombed the Old City with high explosives and incendiary bombs. Large swathes of medieval Bristol were laid waste as historic buildings like the Old Dutch House, the beautiful Elizabethan building of St Peter's Hospital, and St Mary-le-Port Church were destroyed. As the bombers tried to hit the goods yards at Temple Meads railway station, Temple Church nearby was destroyed, although its 800-year-old leaning tower miraculously survived. Temple Street was almost completely obliterated, so that photographs taken next morning remind the viewer of scenes in the war-torn Middle East today. It is because of that night in the Bristol Blitz that this little diamond of a public house, the Cornubia, nestles alone, unseen and often overlooked, dwarfed by the monoliths of post-war concrete office blocks.

A sign painted on the pub's gable end proclaims that it was built around 1775, but it could have been erected somewhat earlier. Once part of a long terrace, it was originally two houses, which are undoubtedly of mid- to late eighteenth-century vintage, with the frontage on the ground floor added when it was converted to a public house at a later date. The left-hand house may once have stood alone as a single inn: its smaller windows date from an earlier period than their larger counterparts on the right. Like the Cornubia's age, the pub's name is something of a mystery. Simeon Pearce, who was a rabbit and game dealer as well as selling beer, had the house in 1853–54 and called it the Rabbit Warren, a name it seems to have retained until 1860, at which time it was definitely called the Cornubia. Anyone who has ever visited Cornwall will know from its ubiquitous flag, a white cross on a black background, that the name for the county in the ancient Britons' Celtic tongue was Kernow. The Roman legions did not penetrate Kernow as completely as they did most of England but their version of the name was Cornubia, so the pub must have had an early connection to the county. James Morgan was the victualler in 1860 and he may have been Cornish, but the most likely link is in the name of a paddle steamer, the SS *Cornubia*.

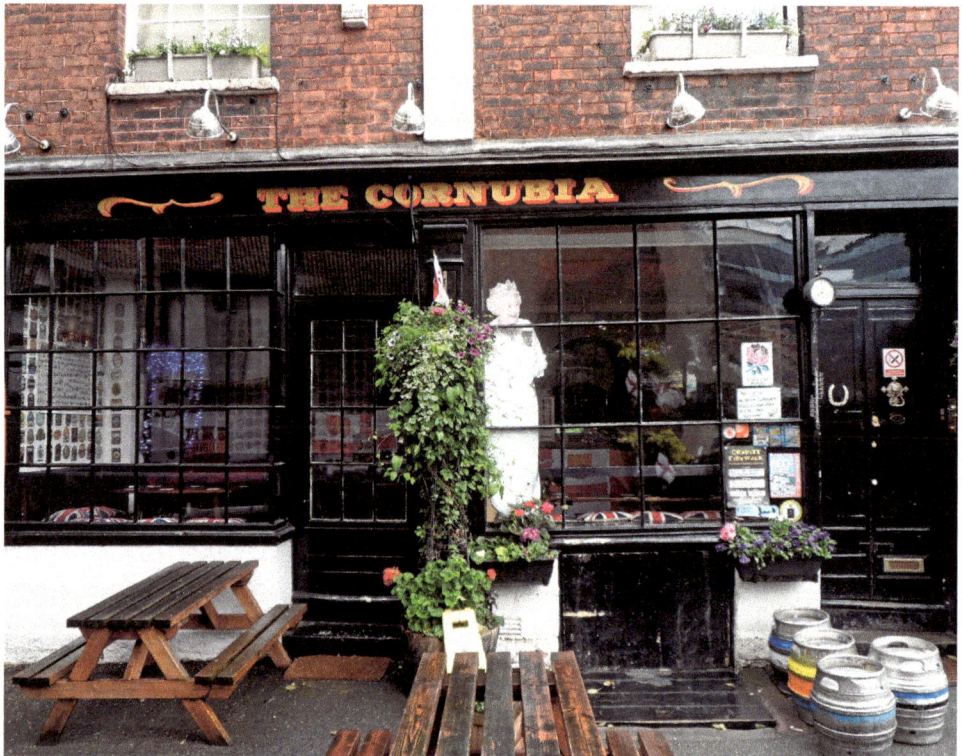

The Cornubia.

There is a pub called the Cornubia Inn in Hayle, Cornwall, whose inn sign depicts this ship painted by the talented artist, Rob Rowland, whose work celebrates the achievements of our industrial heritage. Built in that town 1858, before Isambard Kingdom Brunel's Great Western Railway arrived in west Cornwall, in her early days she was used as a packet ship to carry mail and passengers to Bristol from St Ives. A few years later she was bought by the Confederate side in the American Civil War, who used her as a blockade runner. Eventually she was run aground and captured by the Union, whose officers must have been elated to find waterlogged sacks of mail on board that gave details of Confederate military plans. The ship then became USS *Cornubia* and continued her colourful career on the side of the Yankees.

Bristol's Cornubia is a Real Ale pub, and the panelled walls and ceiling of its pleasant interior are decorated with beer mats from around the UK and beyond. A sign on the door exhorts visitors to 'Beware of the Parrot' but ornithophobia sufferers need have no fear: the bird has been confined to the manager's flat upstairs since its constant swearing upset some of the pub's more sensitive customers.

In 1773 there were eighteen inns and taverns in Temple Street. Around 100 years later, in 1871, there were still fourteen besides the Cornubia: the Mason's Arms, the Duke of Devonshire, the Kings Head, the Dog & Gun, Ye Shakespeare, the Highland Chief, the Cross Guns, the Exeter Tavern, the White Lion, the Bacchus, the Swan, the

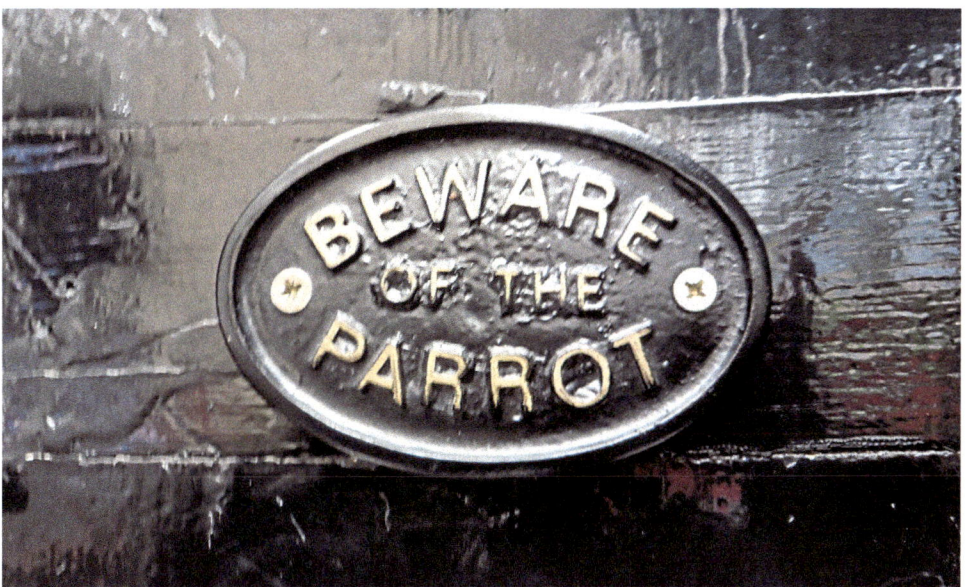

You have been warned!

Lamb & Flag, the Cross Keys and the Crabbe's Well. The last one on the list managed to capitalise on its curious name with the following advertisement: 'The liquor is so good that you will find it as difficult to leave the house as a crab does to get out of a well.'

Besides the Cornubia, only the Kings Head and Ye Shakespeare survive today but they are now in Victoria Street, which was built in 1871 to ease traffic congestion.

27. The Kings Head, Victoria Street

This is a wonderful little pub that is easily overlooked, and that's a shame. The interior is warm and welcoming, with light from the wide front window twinkling cosily on the bottles and glasses behind the bar, and the atmosphere is one that can have changed little for decades. The mahogany bar is original and, unusually these days, has a metal foot-rail running its entire length to increase the comfort of those who prefer to stand as they drink. Behind the bar there is an original, ornate glass mirror lauding the qualities of *Burton Ales and Dublin Stout*, the kind of advertisement that was ripped out of pubs all too often in the 1960s and 1970s, only to be replaced decades later with cheap-looking, unconvincing copies. High in the mahogany shelving beside it there is a feature that I have never seen before. Like all the best ideas it is both simple and ingenious. A brass fixture with slots in it that landlords used in pre-decimal times to check that their old pennies, half-crowns and florins were the genuine article: they would fit a coin into its slot and pull its outer edge down, if it bent it was counterfeit, simple as that.

The Kings Head used to be in Temple Street but the air raid of Sunday 24 November 1940, which left the nearby Cornubia isolated, destroyed what was left of the street. Aiming for the city docks and the freight yards at Temple Meads station, the Luftwaffe used 148 aircraft to drop 12,500 incendiaries and 156 tons of high explosive onto

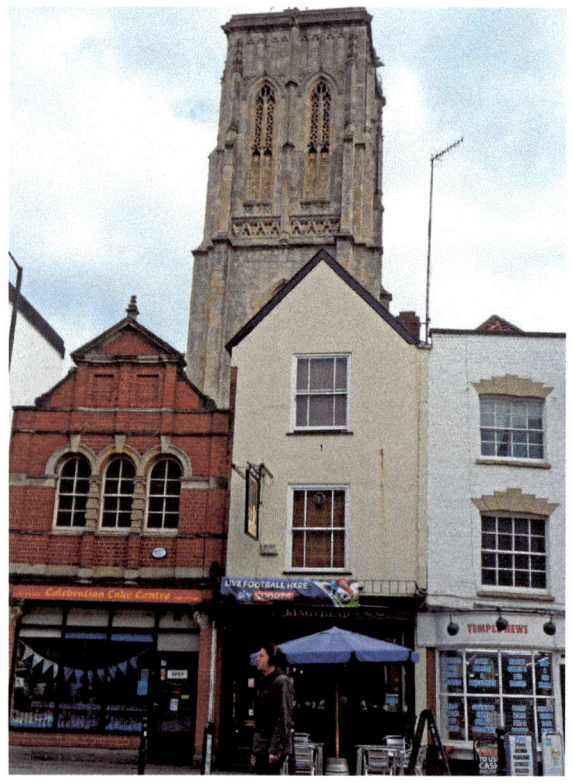

Left: The Kings Head.

Below: Ornate old advertisements.

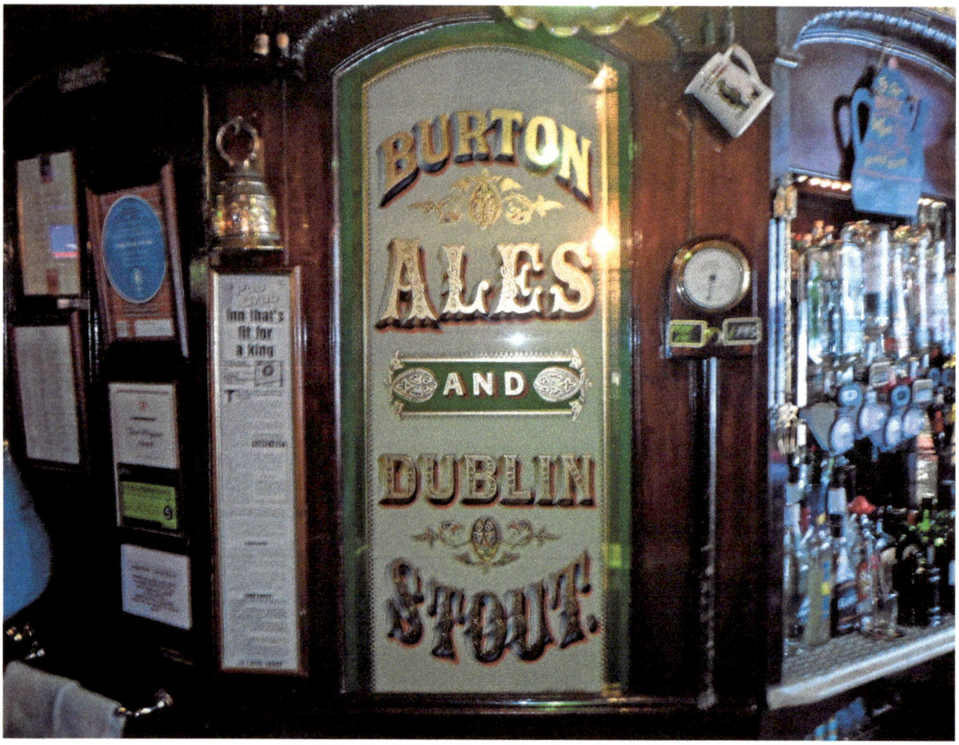

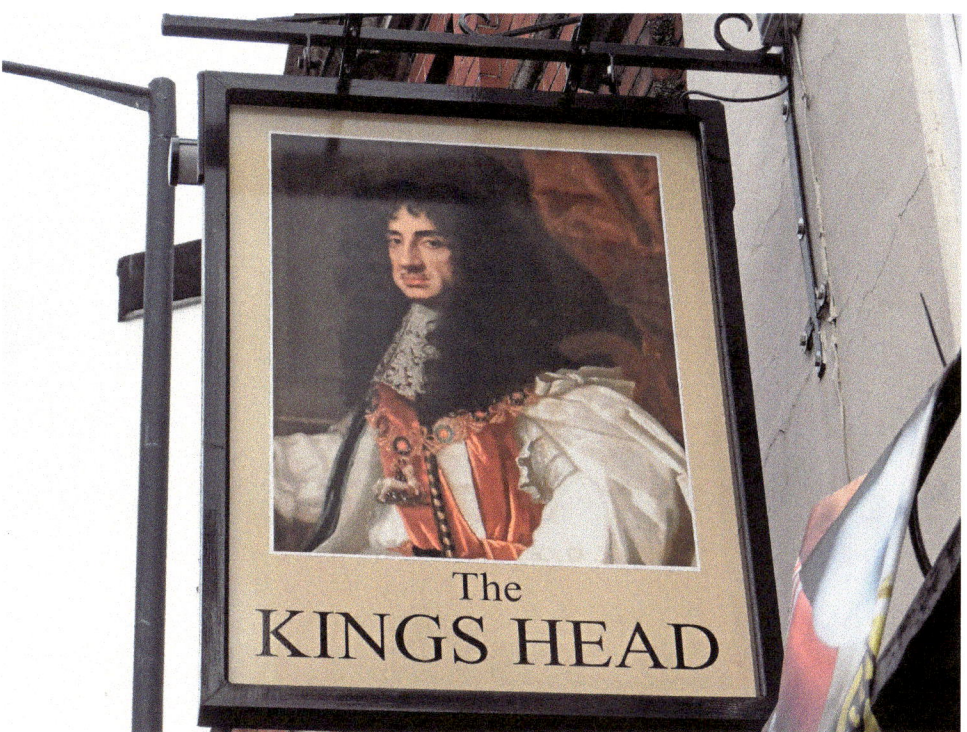

The Kings Head sign.

central Bristol, but failed to eliminate either target. Temple Church, which stands behind the Kings Head, received a direct hit that destroyed its interior, but its tower proved indestructible. For more than six centuries it has been known to Bristolians as the Leaning Tower of Bristol. (Eat your heart out, Pisa!) Its construction began in 1390 but was stopped when it began to lean to one side. Engineering measures were later carried out to correct the fault and the building work resumed in 1459. You can reach Temple Church by stepping out of the back door of the Kings Head, and if you look carefully you will see the point near the top where the tower straightens.

Sadly, the destruction of the area did not stop when hostilities ended. Mindless vandals in the city planning department embarked upon an orgy of demolition, euphemistically labelled 'redevelopment', and this carried on as late as 1974 when they wanted to pull the Kings Head down, along with the two ancient buildings next to it – Nos 62 and 64 Victoria Street. Fortunately, Bristolians had had enough destruction by then and it was the fatuous idea that was scrapped, not this beautiful old pub.

28. Ye Shakespeare, Victoria Street
Surprisingly, there is only one pub called the Shakespeare in the playwright's birthplace of Stratford-upon-Avon while there are two in Bristol. Take care not to confuse our present alehouse, Ye Shakespeare in Victoria Street, with the Shakespeare Tavern in Prince Street, which appeared earlier in this book. Like its near neighbour the

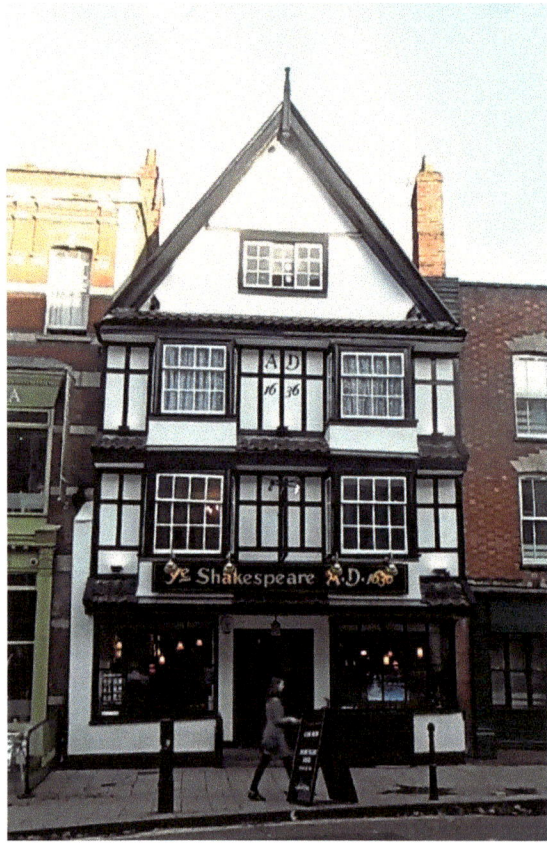

Ye Shakespeare inn.

Kings Head, Ye Shakespeare used to be in Temple Street. There were traffic problems even in the days of horse transport, though, and in 1871 Victoria Street was widened to ease congestion. It absorbed the southern end of Temple Street at the same time, and took these two ancient pubs with it.

The date given on the pub's twentieth-century wall sign is 1636 – twenty years after the Bard's death – and although the style of the timber-framed building has more in common with the merchants' houses built in King Street after 1660, there is little reason to doubt its claim. It is strange that Ye Shakespeare is not mentioned in Sketchley's 1775 directory as one of Temple Street's seventeen inns, some of which I have named in the Cornubia's entry, but that archive does contain omissions and the pub may have been in use as a private house. It could also have been known by a different name, for the names of hostelries changed almost as often in the eighteenth century as they do now.

The wartime bombs that ripped the heart out of nearby Temple Church badly damaged the Shakespeare, but it was restored in the 1950s by a local architect who did great work saving Blitzed Bristol buildings – F. L. Hannam. He was responsible for the splendid two-leaf studded entrance door that adds elegance to the building's front. A lounge was built over the remains of the old brewhouse, where landlords once made their own beer, and its well was found to have almost dried up. Mysteriously, during the course of the restoration a human thigh bone was found within the ancient cellar walls.

29. The Little Grosvenor

A public house is more than a building with people inside it, that description could include a factory or office block, railway station, church or prison. When beer, cider and spirits are added to the mix the public house takes on a human dynamic that is different from all of the above, and can turn into a place almost of magic. So while you may have passed this apparently insignificant corner pub on the Cut, whose most significant feature in your mind might be its closeness to the Asda car park, and thought it a little rundown or drab, if you go inside and sit for a while you may sense something warm and human that you did not expect.

The Grosvenor's customers are overwhelmingly working class with many drawn from the nearby council housing blocks around Redcliffe Hill, struggling to get by on state benefits or barely adequate pensions. Years of unrelenting manual labour have taken their toll on some, so that men who are not very old but are nevertheless tottering about on walking sticks or mobility aids are not as unusual as they should be. Although the clientele are rough and ready, theirs is generally a caring attitude towards these casualties of a hard life, and you will often see them being helped with great consideration. Some of the women customers look as though they have walked straight out of a Beryl Cook painting, and it comes as no surprise that that artist lived for many years in Bristol, drawing early inspiration from the city. Rough

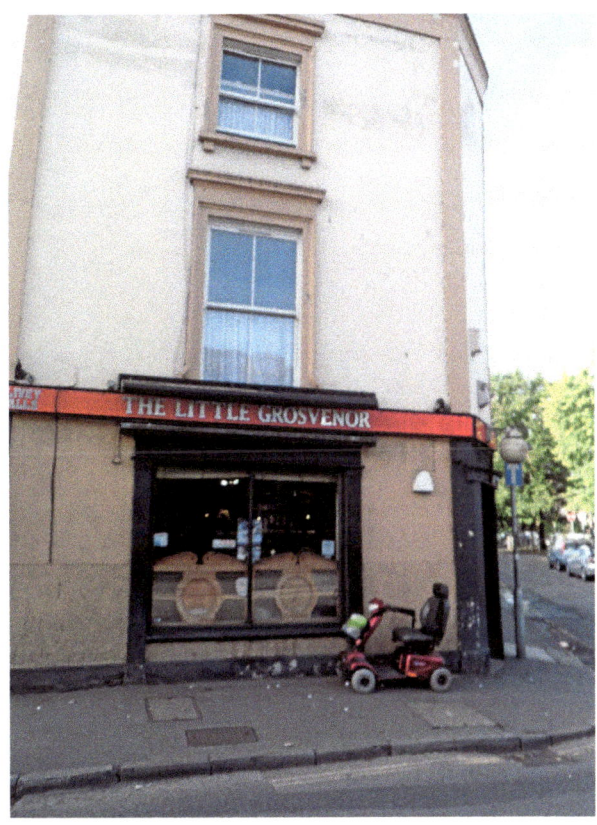

The Little Grosvenor.

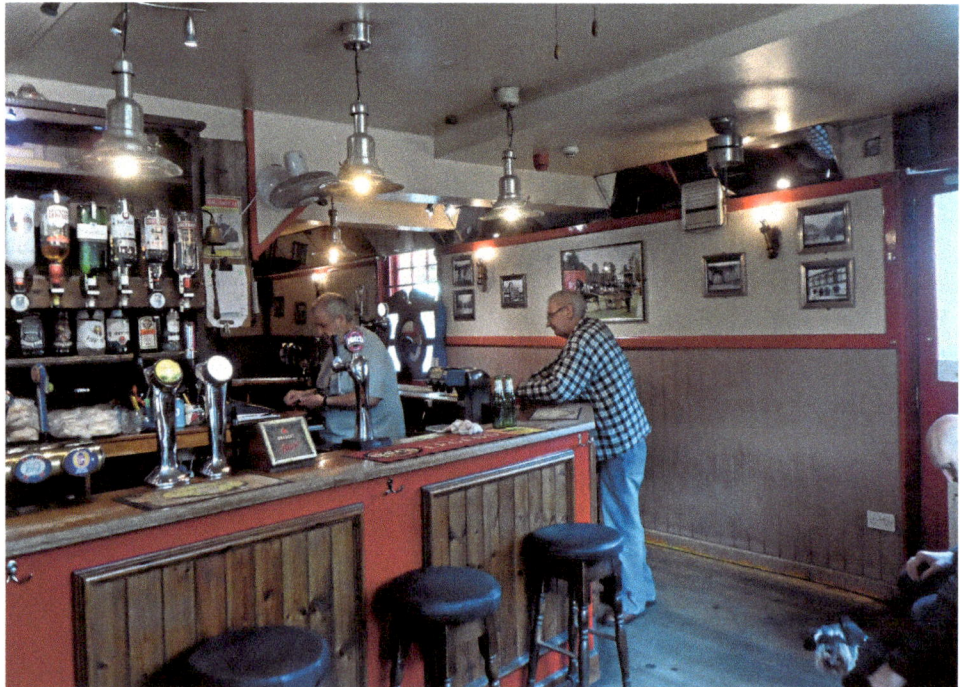

Bar of the Little Grosvenor.

cider is a favourite tipple, with Thatcher's Traditional, 6% in strength and unchanged since Edwardian times, vying for popularity with the Bass Ale that, sadly, is becoming increasingly hard to find nowadays. There is a covered smoking area at the rear, and when the weather is cold the tobacco addicts cluster around its doorway and try to insinuate their way back into the pub, only to be driven out again by buxom barmaids.

The music is usually loud and impromptu dances often happen, with dancers perhaps in pairs, perhaps in groups, or just expressing themselves alone; in the relaxed atmosphere of the Little Grosvenor it simply does not matter. An unwelcome result of the pub's nearness to the Asda supermarket and East Street's shops is that, despite the vigilance of the staff, it is sometimes troubled by shoplifters trying to sell pilfered goods. For reasons I have never been able to fathom there is a chalked board on the bar giving the number of shopping days to the festive season; recently someone rubbed out 'shopping' and altered the sign to say, 'Only 251 shoplifting days to Christmas.'

30. The Apple Tree, Philip Street

If the name is not enough, the picture of an apple tree laden with fruit on the outside wall of this tiny backstreet boozer should alert even the most obtuse drinker to the fact that cider rather than beer is the staple here – though it keeps John Smith's and other beers on tap. In past times, Bristol's closeness to the orchards of Somerset ensured that there were many Apple Tree pubs in the city, with one in Broadmead, another in Thomas Street, a third and fourth in Albert Street and on Midland Road in St Philips, as

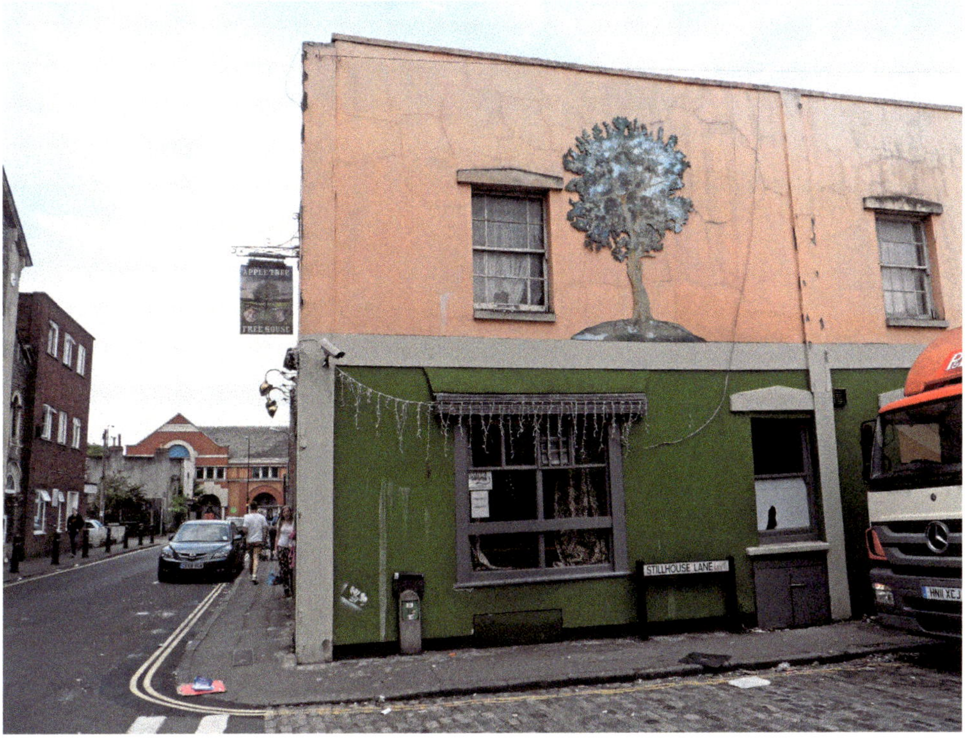

Above: The Apple Tree.

Right: Apple Tree sign.

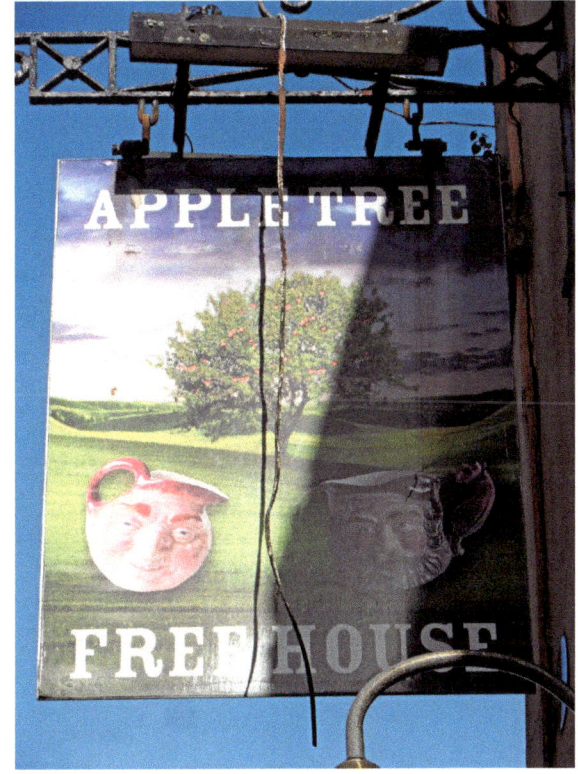

well as a fifth and six in the area of Great Gardens, which vanished in 1913, flattened to extend the goods yards at Temple Meads. There was even one around the corner from Philip Street on Bedminster Parade but this did not cause confusion as the present Apple Tree was then called the Maltster's Arms. In 1871, the landlord at the Maltster's was George Winstone Broad and from 1944 until 1953 the pub was held by Leonard King. It was probably when Leonard retired that the pub took its present name.

There is hardly space to swing a teabag inside the single room of the bar and the décor cannot have changed for decades, but I have always found the Apple Tree intriguing. Some of the customers may look as rough as the Taunton Traditional and Cheddar Valley ciders on sale, but the general attitude towards strangers in one of friendly curiosity despite the sign that reads, 'Only locals after 8pm'. The garden beside the pub may look, during the winter months, like Hiroshima after the atom bomb, but there is music there in the summer and I find it a pleasant place to escape to when my wife tries to drag me around the shops in East Street.

31. The Avon Packet Tavern, Southville
Anyone who ever drives along Coronation Road beside the Cut, which means just about everyone in Bristol, knows this pub because its landlord has had the good

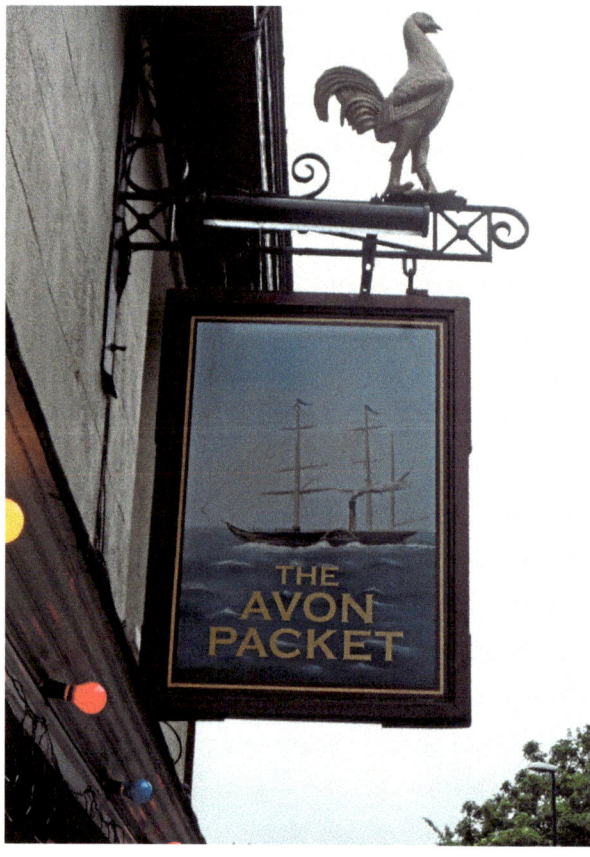

The Avon Packet sign.

business sense to attract attention to it by hanging a string of multicoloured lights outside that shine both day and night. The tavern dates from 1820, when it was converted from three old cottages at Nos 185, 186 and 187 Coronation Road. At that time, though, it had a different name that has now been forgotten. The pub almost certainly gained its present title in 1834 when the War Office Packet Company, which had been so named since 1823, reinvented itself as the New Steam Packet Co. Pleasure craft taking day trippers from Bristol to Bristol Channel ports like Ilfracombe and Barry were popular from Victorian times and remain so today, although they are now rarer and limited to the MV *Balmoral*. In 1809, after William Jessop created the floating harbour that ended the days when ships arriving at the port of Bristol were unloaded while beached in the mud, it is likely that some sailed from a jetty on the New Cut itself, into which the tidal River Avon had been diverted. Moses Evans was the landlord in 1851, and on the eve of the Second World War in 1939 the licensee, Stanley Stone, paid an annual rent of £90 to George's Brewery.

Inside, the pub is a pleasant, characterful place in the welcoming public house tradition that has served drinkers well for centuries. The bar has scores or perhaps hundreds of keyrings on display that drinkers must have contributed over the decades,

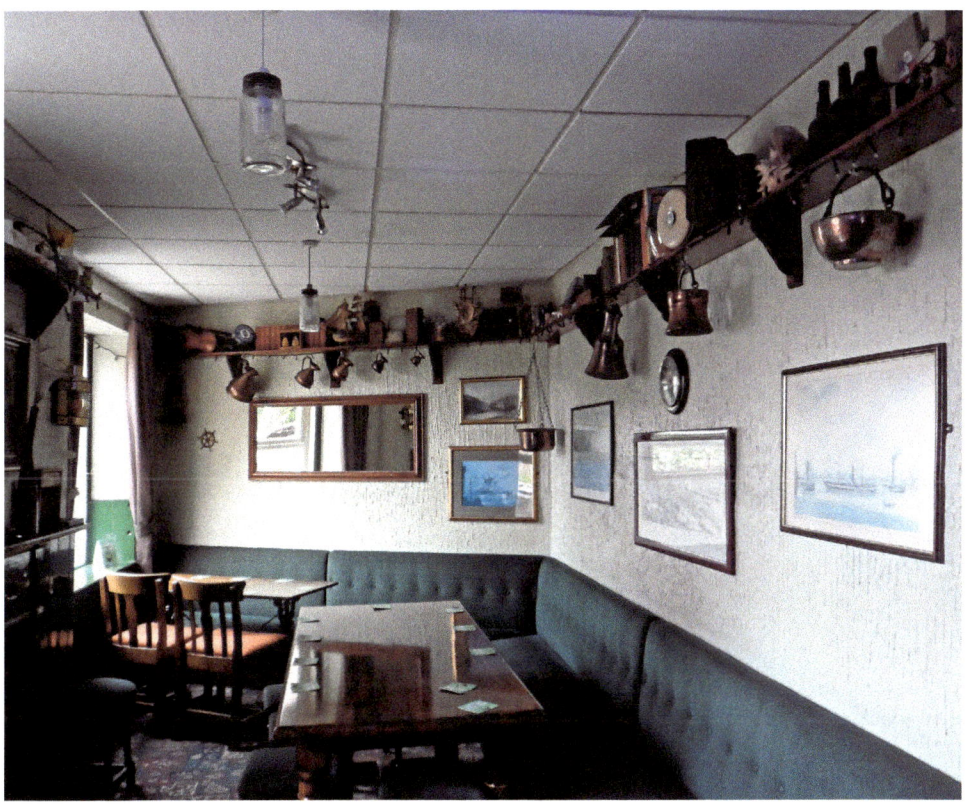

The Avon Packet lounge.

and the walls in the back room are adorned with pictures of a nautical flavour and shelves crammed with interesting curios, useful for providing a talking point to fill the awkward silences that can happen on a first date. There is a garden at the rear, which is such a pleasant spot to enjoy a tipple that you would never guess it has a grim history and was once a pit, used for the cruel so-called sport of bear-baiting.

32. The Miners Arms, Bedminster Down Road

The only remnants of a once-dominant coal industry that remain in Bedminster today are the Shepton footbridge over the railway, the Jolly Colliers pub in West Street and the Miners Arms on Bedminster Down Road. Those of us who are lucky enough to live in the area may not realise it, but our homes and the pavements we walk upon daily stand over a maze-like honeycomb of old mine workings from earlier times, when Bedminster's coal fuelled Bristol's industrial revolution. The Smyths, lords of the Ashton Court manor, owned all the mineral rights in the land around and their mines extended from Bedminster Down to beneath the River Avon. Long Ashton had the first pit in the 1720s and the South Liberty Colliery, which opened twenty years later, was the last to close, in 1920.

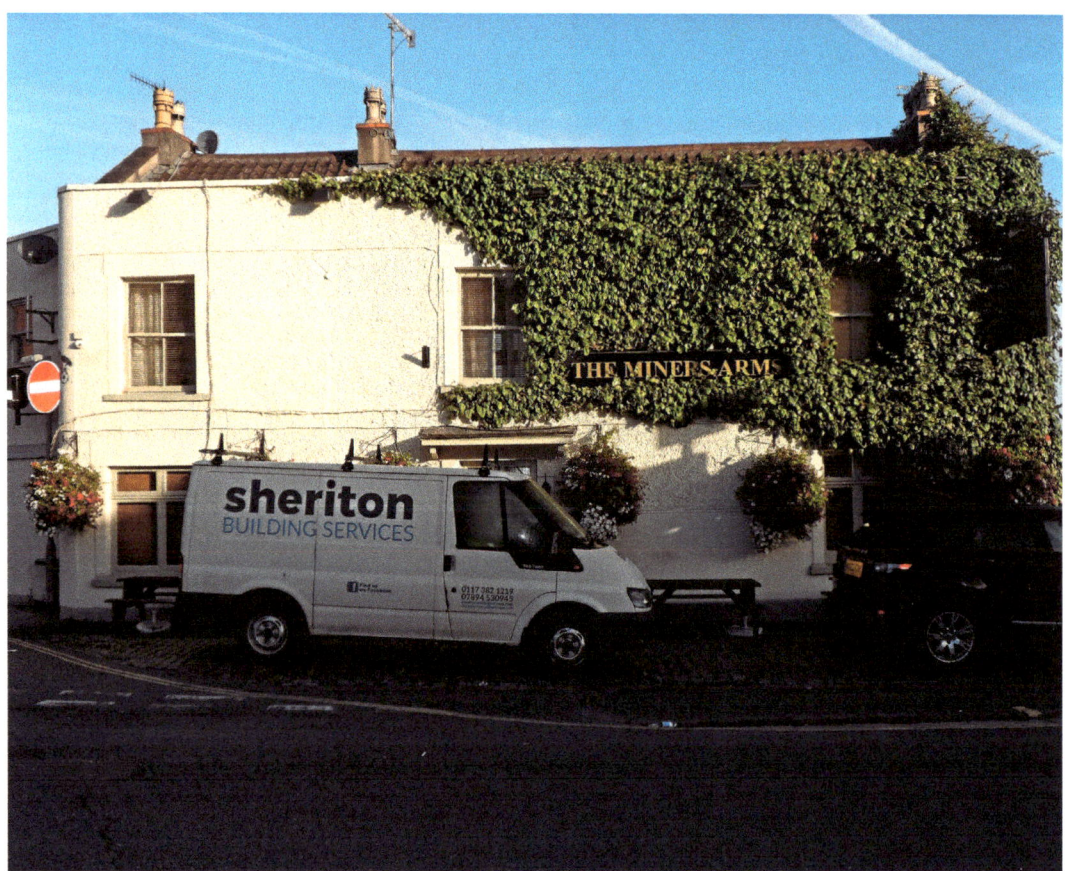

The Miners Arms.

A sign painted on the pub's southerly wall saying, 'Welcome to South Bristol', is the first indication to new arrivals from Bristol Airport that they have arrived in the city proper, and they could do far worse than stop-off at this friendly, traditional local whose landlord knows what people want from a pub. A blazing log fire in the winter months gives the place a warm ambience. There are widescreen TVs showing live sports, a side room with a pool table, and for those who want peace or a degree of privacy, a large, snug-like room at the back from where you can see the Clifton suspension bridge, lit up at night like a glowing necklace tossed over the Avon Gorge. There is a beer garden at the rear, and picnic tables at the front of the pub from which you can watch the cars gliding around a one-way traffic system that would spell the doom of a pub held in less capable hands. The range of beers, lagers and cider on sale include locally brewed Butcombe bitter, John Smith's, Stella Artois in stemmed pint glasses and Thatcher's Gold, while a poster outside proclaiming 'Bristol Born and Red' leaves no-one in any doubt of this pub's unfailing loyalty to Bristol City Football Club.

A real family pub, the Miners Arms welcomes children and dogs as your author can testify personally – he has both.

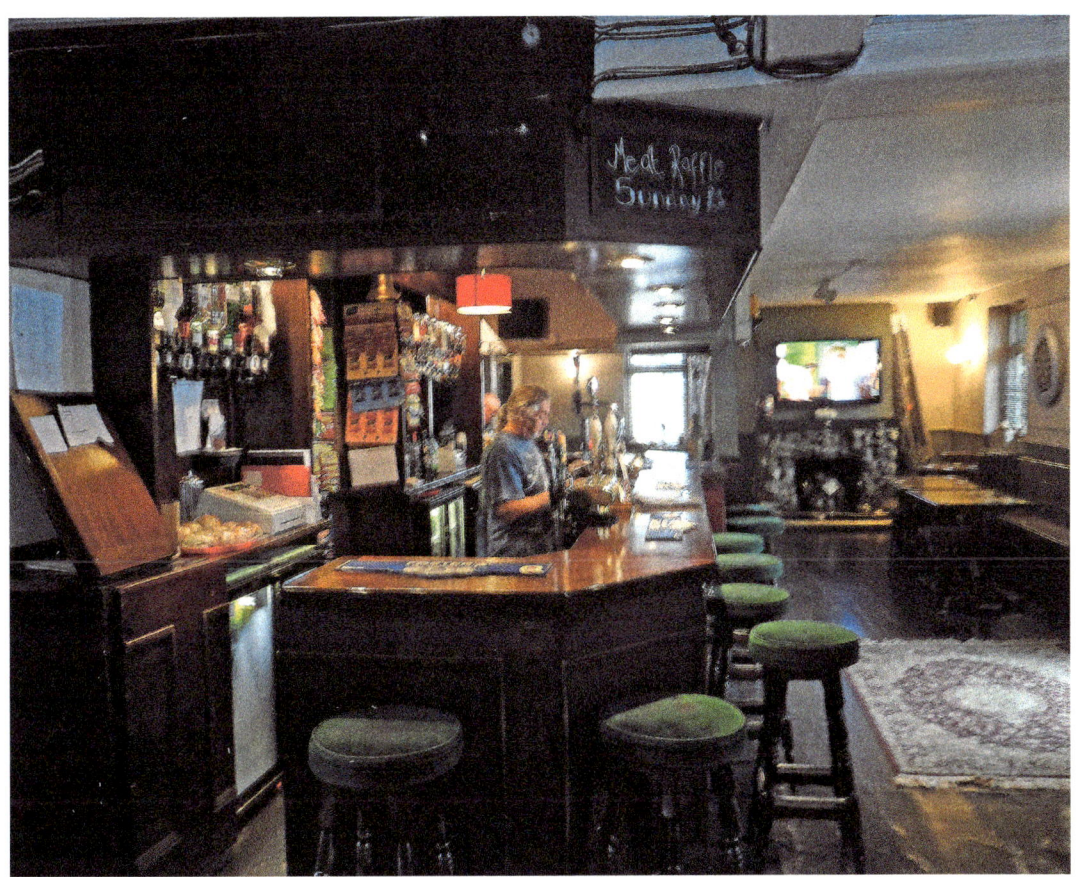

The Miners Arms lounge.

4

East

33. The Stag & Hounds, Old Market Street
Like its near neighbour, the Long Bar, this old pub was built in the 1600s, although in its case it may have been a case of total refurbishment rather than new build. A courthouse once stood on the spot and parts of it may remain within the fabric of the present

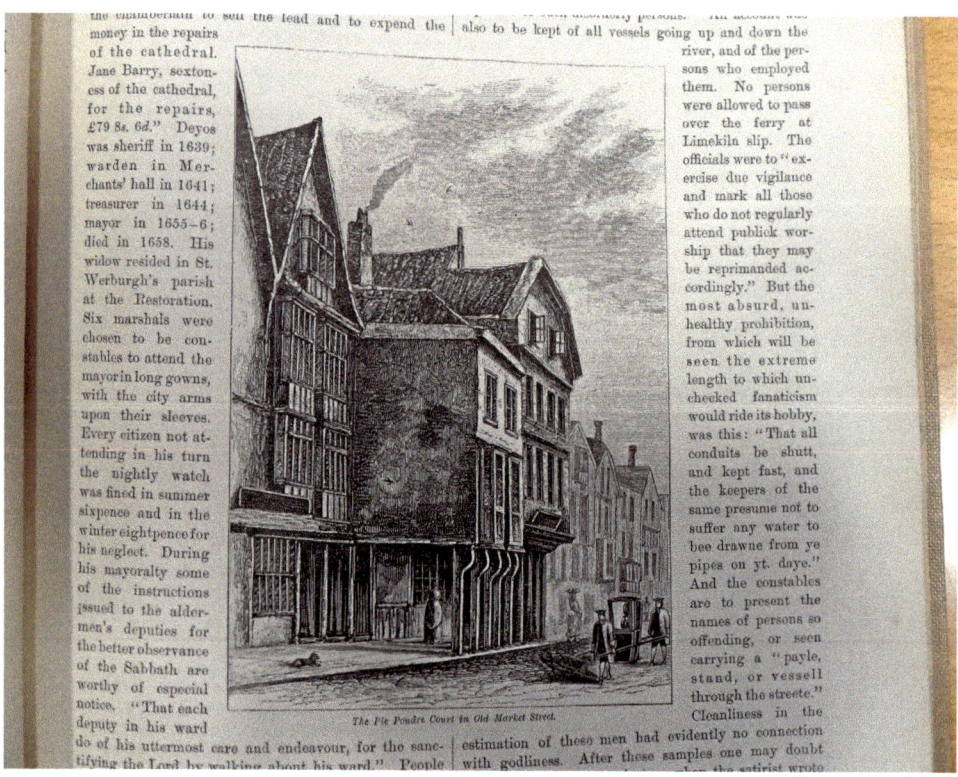

The Pie Poudre court.

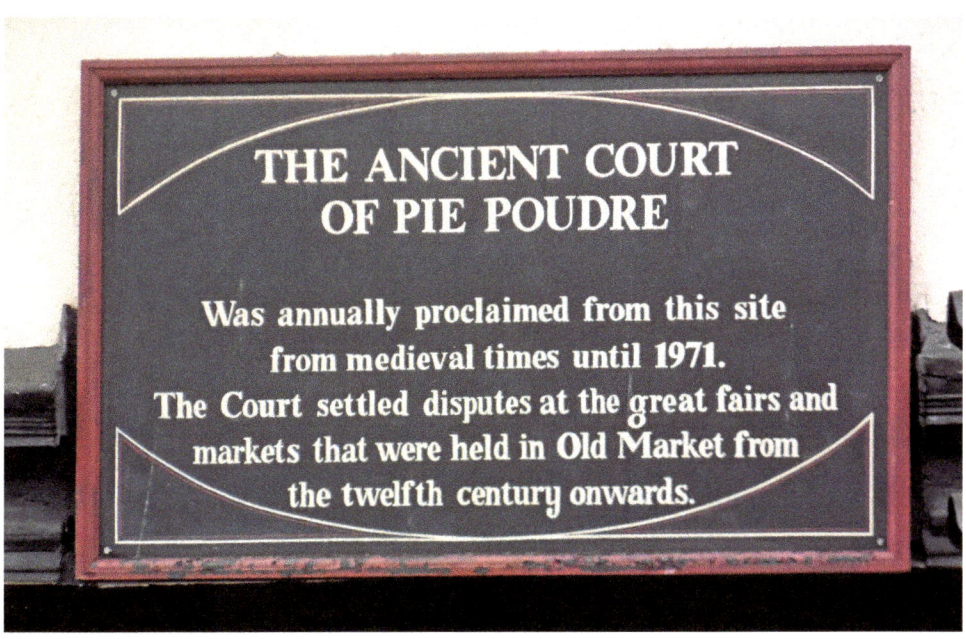

Stag & Hounds sign.

building. The first suburb to appear outside the ancient walled city of Bristol was its market area, close to the walls of the Norman castle and a place where corn, cattle and all kinds of other goods were bought and sold, and food and drink were plentiful. Not surprisingly, the market attracted crime and drunkenness so a court was set up that dealt out summary justice so swiftly, it was said, that the dust did not have time to settle on the miscreants' feet. The court became known as the Court of the Pie Poudre, as 'pied-poudre' meant 'dusty feet' in Norman French. The court had an opening ceremony each year until 1870, when the annual disturbances that accompanied it resulted in its dissolution, although a more muted opening ceremony carried on as a memorial until 1973. Nowadays, only a plaque on the pub wall commemorates the event.

The building, with its casement upper windows and its first floor supported by four simple pillars to make a shelter over the pavement, is both attractive and unusual, although the house at No. 59 was built in the same style and there may have been others in the past that have not survived. Most old alehouses retain little of interest inside, and in this respect the Stag & Hounds is lucky in terms of fixtures. There is a wonderful Jacobean seventeenth-century staircase whose ornate, twisted balusters reminded your author of the drunkard's staircase at the Full Moon. There is also seventeenth-century wood panelling on the first floor that has remained in first class condition.

In an outhouse across the rear yard there remains a Victorian pumping apparatus that once brought water to the inn, probably from a depth of 9 metres, around 100 feet in old measurements. Looking out at the back of the pub is a tiny window said to belong to a priest's hole, accessible via a trapdoor in a bathroom ceiling. Doubt has been cast on the validity of this claim since these hiding places date from the second

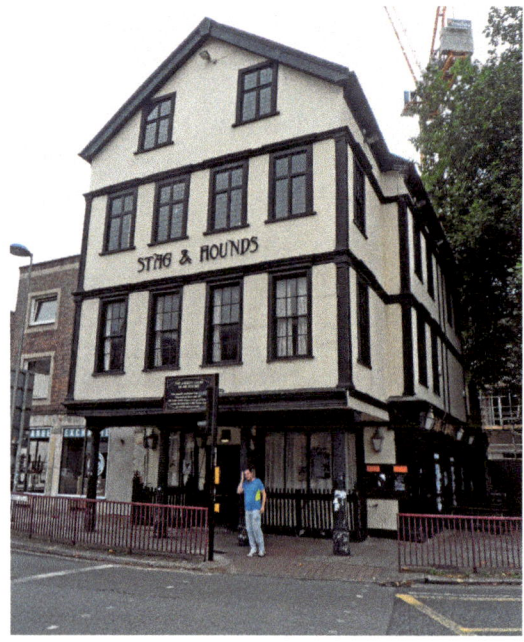

The Stag & Hounds.

half of the sixteenth century, when it was treason for a priest to enter England and Catholic families built priest holes into their houses so as to conceal them. Whatever be the truth of it, the Stag & Hounds is a fine old pub. Its landlord in 1792 was William Prowlin. Joseph Perret, licensee in 1836, was still there twenty-six years later despite also having a soap boiling business in nearby Castle Street.

34. The Long Bar, Old Market

This half-timbered building is typical of the houses built for wealthy Bristol merchants in the late seventeenth century, and is believed to have been erected in 1670. It has some unusual original features, like the pierced bargeboards that protect the gable ends and the frilled woodwork that marks the division of each floor, adding character to the building that would look far taller without them. The present entrance must have been added afterwards as the wooden trusses beside the door are typical of a later period. The house did not continue as a private dwelling, and had certainly become an inn by 1752 when William Streeter was recorded as its landlord, succeeded in 1764 by James Pike. In these earlier times the Long Bar had a tap room in front, looking out onto Old Market, and the area near its entrance still retains the feel of that. Stables at the rear were reached via Jacob Street, and like virtually all alehouses in those days, it had a brewhouse where it made its own ale. A smoke room and bar completed the picture, and doubtless accommodation was offered on the upper floors. Recently this old pub has begun to restyle itself as the Cider House, although the name of the Long Bar remains proudly on its outer wall.

Despite the distinctive length of its bar, for many decades the pub was called the Three Horseshoes. During some of that time, and certainly up until the 1930s, it was the haunt of acts from the Empire theatre, which stood nearby. This music hall, which

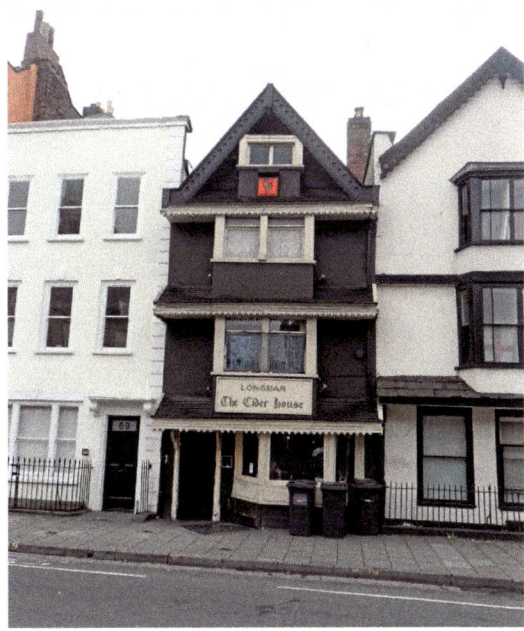

The Long Bar.

styled itself a 'palace of varieties', provided the Hollywood heartthrob Cary Grant with his first job in show business as a lime-lighter, shining a beam of bright light onto performers like Little Tich, Flanagan and Allen, Gracie Fields and the early drag act, Old Mother Riley. In the late nineteenth and early twentieth centuries the Long Bar was known locally as the House of Refreshment. Burlesque acts from the Empire are known to have given impromptu performances in the pub, probably for free drinks.

35. The Palace Hotel, West Street

Gin became the favourite drink of the common people in the 1700s, mainly because it is derived from juniper berries, which grow in England and so could be made cheaply, without the expense of importation like its rivals, brandy and rum. The first gin palaces were built in London in the 1820s, and the drunkenness and debauchery they brought with them was so great that their name still lingers in the public consciousness, with the result that this Grade II-listed Victorian building, which still retains many of its original fixtures and fittings, is known locally as the Gin Palace. When building was started in 1869 it was believed that it would be next to the Great Western Railway's new terminus, but John Sharp, landlord when it opened in 1871, was in for a disappointment. The plan was changed and Isambard Kingdom Brunel built his new station at nearby Temple Meads instead.

The Palace is striking by any standards. The front of the building has a balcony flanked by a pair of atlantes supporting the roof with its large clock, a throwback to its roots as a railway hotel. The interior is no less ornate. The front bar, which was intended as the hotel's reception area, still has its original Victorian mirrors and supporting twisted brass 'barley sugar' pillars, which make it a wonder to behold. Most buildings constructed on the side of a hill have their floors made level, but the Gin Palace is an exception to this

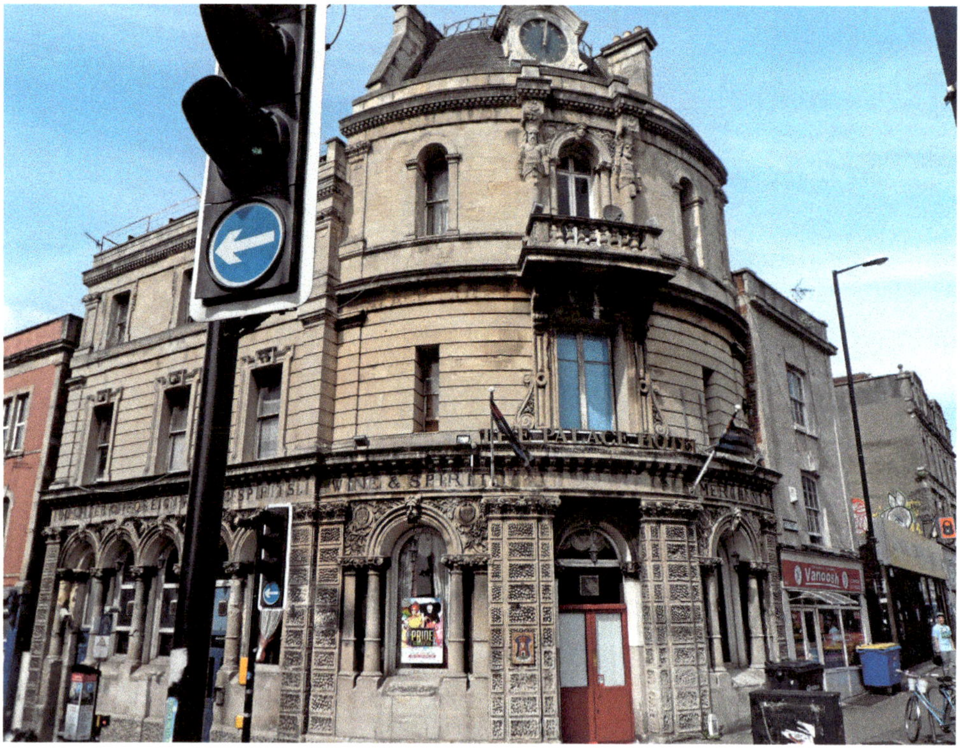

Above: The Palace Hotel.

Below: The Palace Atlantes.

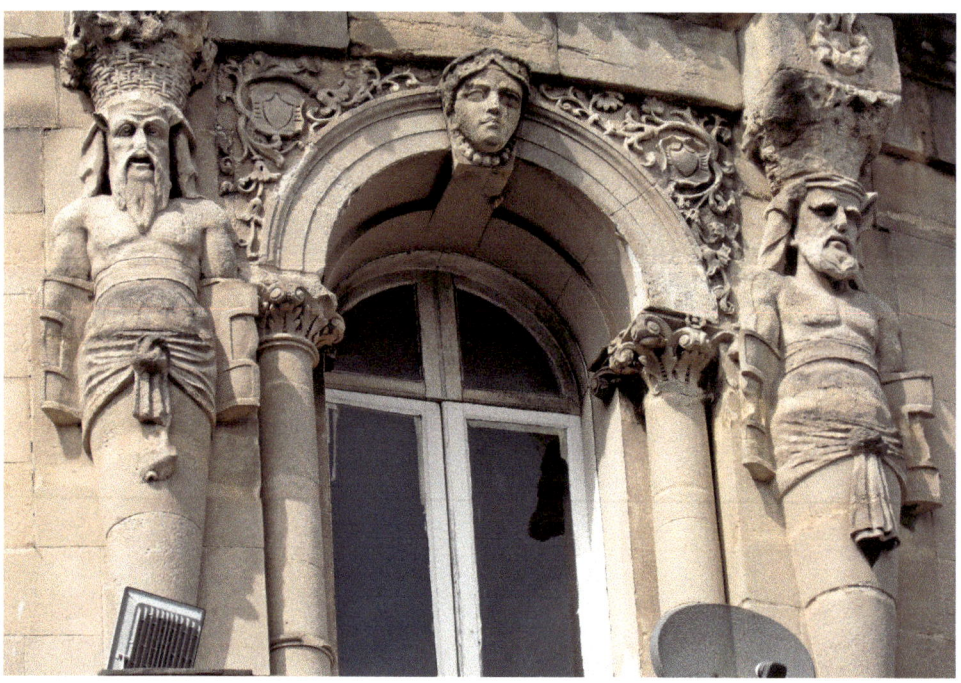

rule: the floor in the front bar has a distinct slope, apparently retained to aid the railway porters' trolleys that never in fact materialised there, which can be disconcerting to those who have had a drink or three. Designed by Henry Masters, creator of the Boardroom pub in St Nicholas Street that used to be a gay bar called the Elephant, the Palace is now a popular gay venue in the Old Market pink village. Don't let that put you off if you're straight, the pub does not discriminate but provides a warm welcome to all.

36. The Packhorse, Lawrence Hill

The Packhorse nowadays is a favourite haunt of bikers. If some readers view it with trepidation as a result, I would like to assure them that I found it a friendly place. It stands on Lawrence Hill, which has been on the main Bristol to London road since Roman times. The first known tavern at the spot was built in the mid-1700s and was probably also an inn, accommodating merchants and other travellers on the country lanes that then criss-crossed the area. Ducie Road was called Packhorse Lane at that time and the inn property included stables and a brewery at the rear. Thomas Crisp was landlord in 1792 but in 1800 the property was taken over by William Herapath. His son, also called William, gained an interest in chemistry while working in the brewery, left the business to study it, and was instrumental in setting up both the Chemical Society of London and Bristol Medical School. He was also responsible for the first forensic exhumation in Britain when the corpse of Clara Ann Smith was disinterred fourteen months after her death, and he found large amounts of arsenic in her stomach. Mary Anne Burdock, who had killed the wealthy woman while she was living in the lodging house she ran, was convicted as a

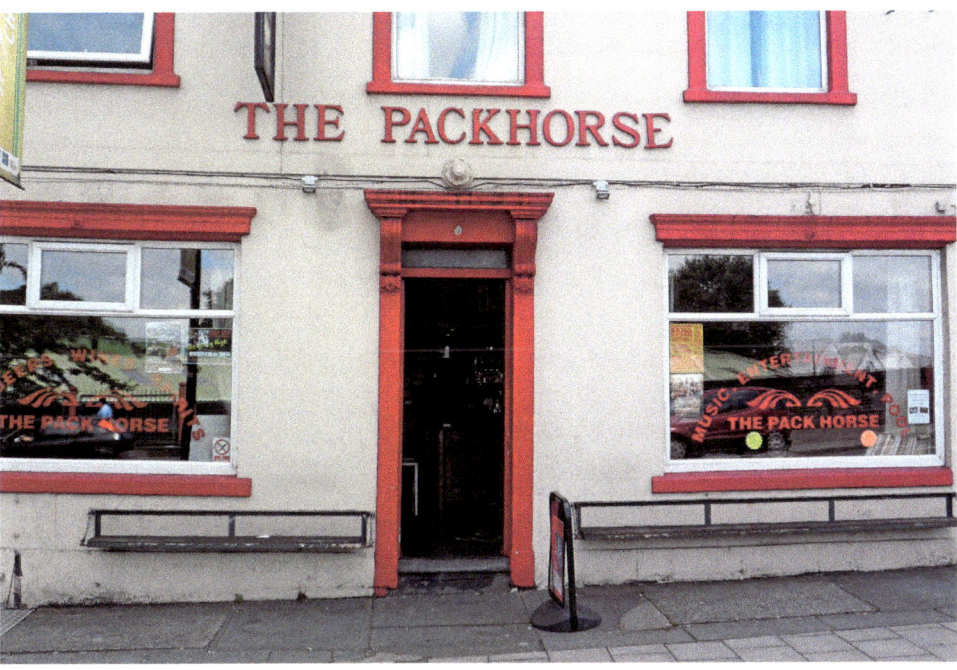

The Packhorse.

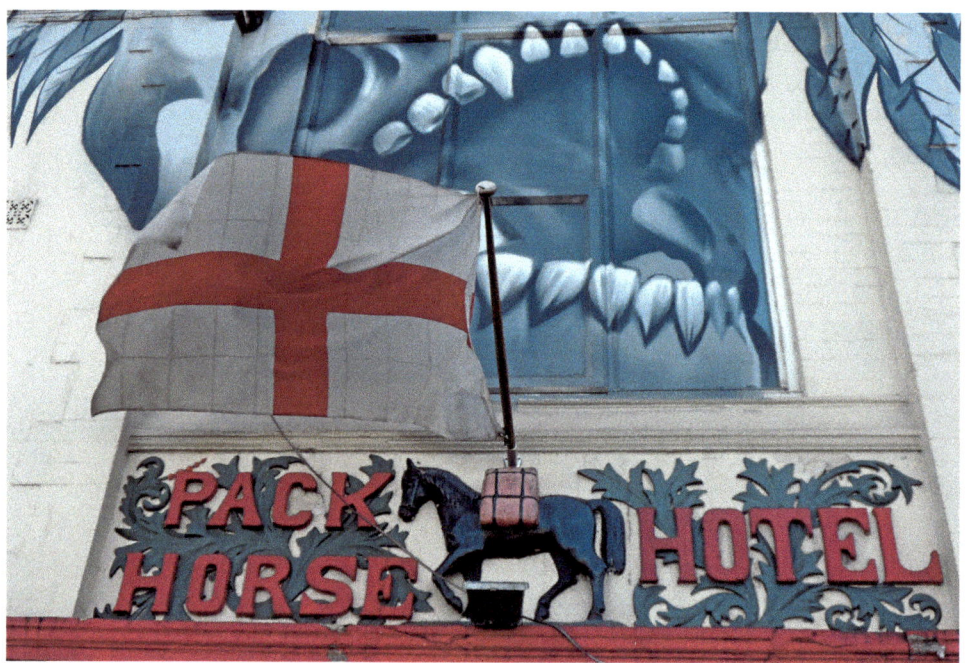

Splendid sign at The Packhorse.

result and became known as 'the Bristol Poisoner'. Burdock was hanged on the gatehouse of the New Gaol in Cumberland Road, watched by an estimated crowd of 50,000.

Strangely, today's entrance door at the Packhorse used to be on the first floor while the original inn still lies below. In 1832, a horse-drawn railway ran beside the Packhorse over a wooden bridge, but when the Bristol & Gloucester Railway arrived in 1879 they built a new bridge so that the pub and its neighbouring shops disappeared under stone arches. As a result, the original parts of the pub are now hidden. In the early days several tunnels leading to the cobbled streets of shops, still with glass in their windows and with gas lamps standing outside them, could be reached by venturing into the Packhorse's cellars. In the 1960s, these entrances were bricked up with concrete blocks, so that to this day a complete Victorian shopping area lies frozen in time beneath Lawrence Hill, waiting for archaeologists of the future to find and restore it.

37. The Rhubarb Tavern, Barton Hill

This pub is tucked away on little-used Queen Ann Road in Barton Hill, and looking around at the towering high-rise council blocks that dominate the area today it is difficult to envisage it as a rural place of fields and country lanes, remote from Bristol. Yet until industry began to move into Barton Hill in the late 1830s that is exactly what it was. As so often happens, there was an older tavern on the same spot. This began life in the 1600s as a farmhouse surrounded by fields of rhubarb, which, surprisingly, was still grown as a commercial crop in Barton Hill in the mid-1940s. Parts of the old inn still remain in the fabric of the Rhubarb Tavern we see today whose front was added

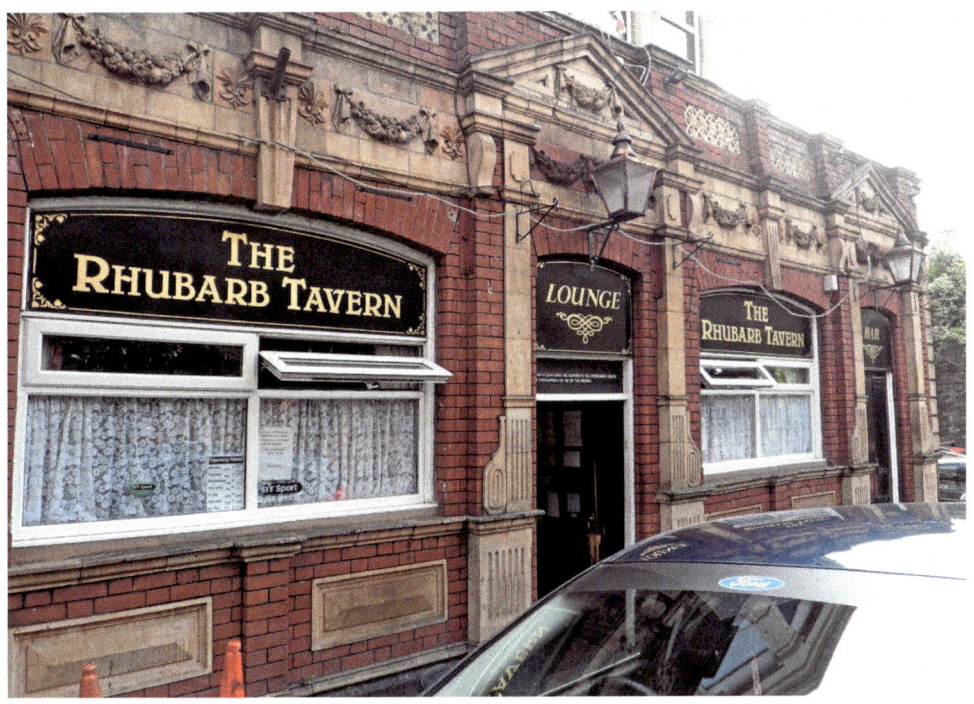

Above: The Rhubarb Tavern.

Below: Rhubarb fireplace.

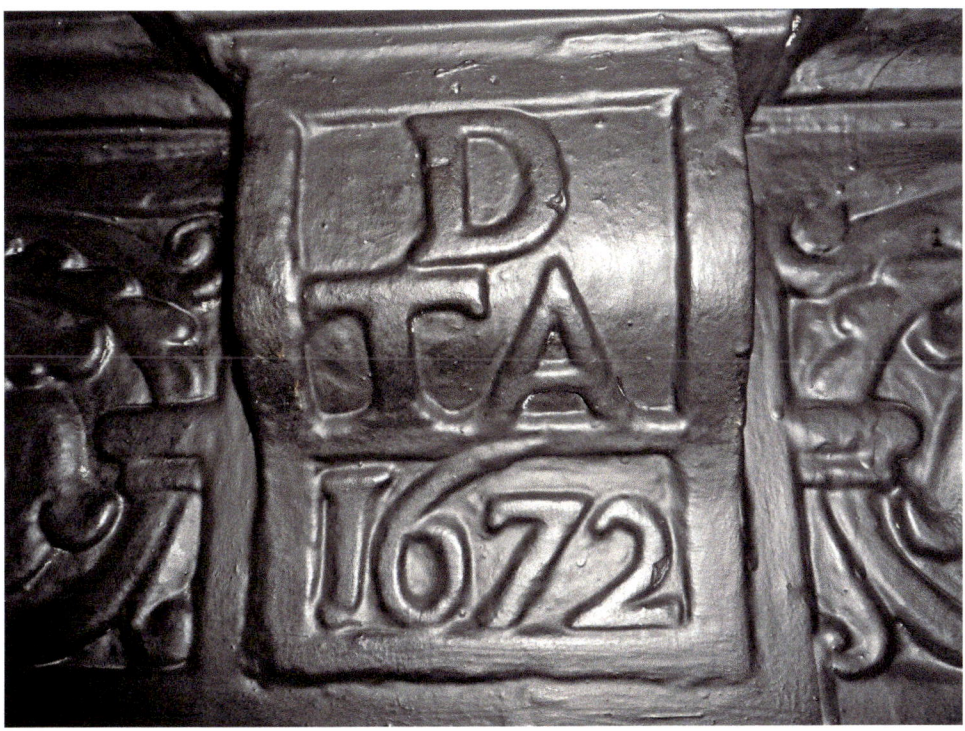

later, probably in the early nineteenth century. While the pub's name is not unique it is certainly rare: I could only trace two, both are in Yorkshire and also stand in areas that once raised crops of rhubarb.

In the back room of the Rhubarb Tavern there is a carved seventeenth-century stone fireplace bearing the initials 'D. A. T.' and the date '1672'. This did not originally belong to the pub but was taken from Tilly Court, the mansion of Sir Thomas A. Day, which once stood opposite. Sir Thomas, a wealthy manufacturer of soap for whom nearby Days Road is named, was mayor of Bristol in 1687–88, and as well as his country seat in the Barton he had a magnificent townhouse on Bristol Bridge. Queen Anne once dined there, and it seems that with the passage of time this event was mistakenly ascribed to Tilly Court, with the result that the street where it stood was misnamed Queen Anne Road.

In 1871 the Rhubarb Tavern's landlord was Thomas Church, and there was a rumour that a tunnel ran from its back garden down to the Feeder canal. If you look closely at the gable wall you will just about make out the name of the older Bristol brewery, *Georges & Co.*, still visible in ghostly letters. The pub's interior is pleasant, the landlady is friendly and the garden has picnic tables and a small, covered stage for music events.

38. The Farm, St Werburgh's

I arrived in Bristol from the Costa del Mersey in the winter of 1976, on a night of the thick fog we still had in those days, believing I would only stay for a weekend. Dropped-off in the city centre, it took me hours to find St Werburgh's, and even then

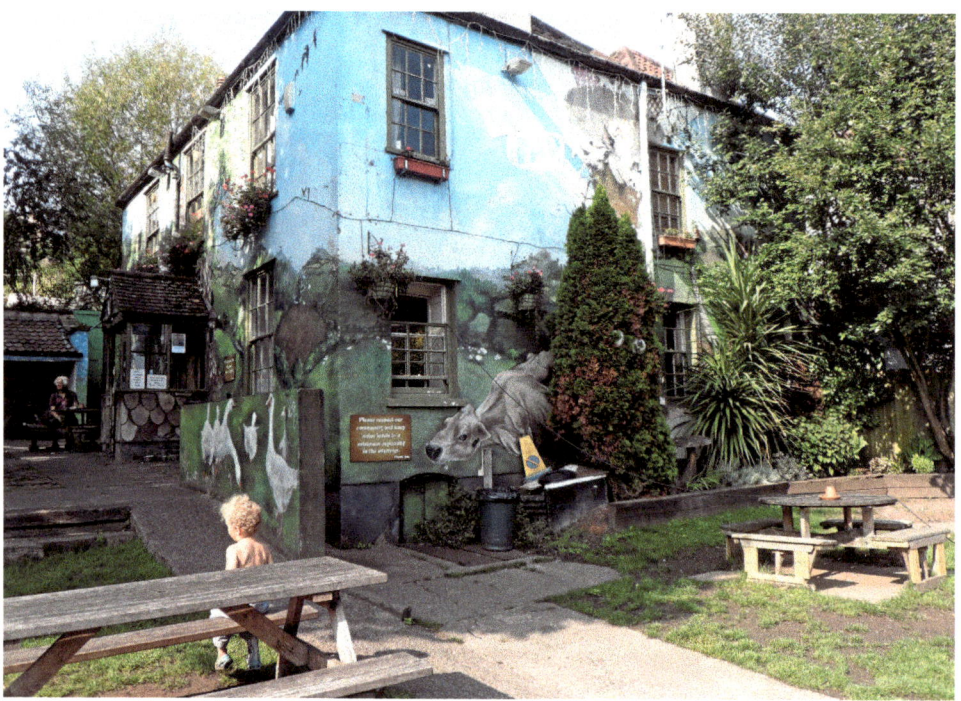

The Farm.

I had to grope my way along an ill-lit railway tunnel to Hopetoun Road and the house where I was to stay. It wasn't until next day that I discovered the odd little pub that also occupied the street, which turned out to be a kind of licensed time machine. To lift its old-fashioned latch and enter the bar was to be transported back to the 1930s, to a place of cream-painted walls rendered a filthy yellowish-brown by generations of tobacco smoke, where ancient Bristolians coughed and spat as they put the world to rights over pints of flat beer. The only decoration was a picture, torn roughly from the *Evening Post* and fixed onto the wall at a crazy angle with wilting adhesive tape, of an elephant at Bristol Zoo urinating. The pub was called the South Wales Railway Tavern in those days because, like the Palace Hotel, it had been opened in the expectation of a railway stop that never actually materialised, but local people always called it The Farm. It undoubtedly had been a farmhouse at some time in the past, the open-ended outhouses near the entrance door were in fact old pigsties and they are still there today, with seats and rough tables inside, providing shelter for drinkers when wind or rain rule out sitting on what is now a pleasant lawn.

Coincidentally, the 1970s licensees had once run the previous pub featured in this book, the Rhubarb Tavern in Barton Hill, so they must have had a penchant for the out of the way and rundown. They were incredibly – but truthfully – named Bill and Gladys Grubb. When the place was empty, which it often was, a rap on the bar would

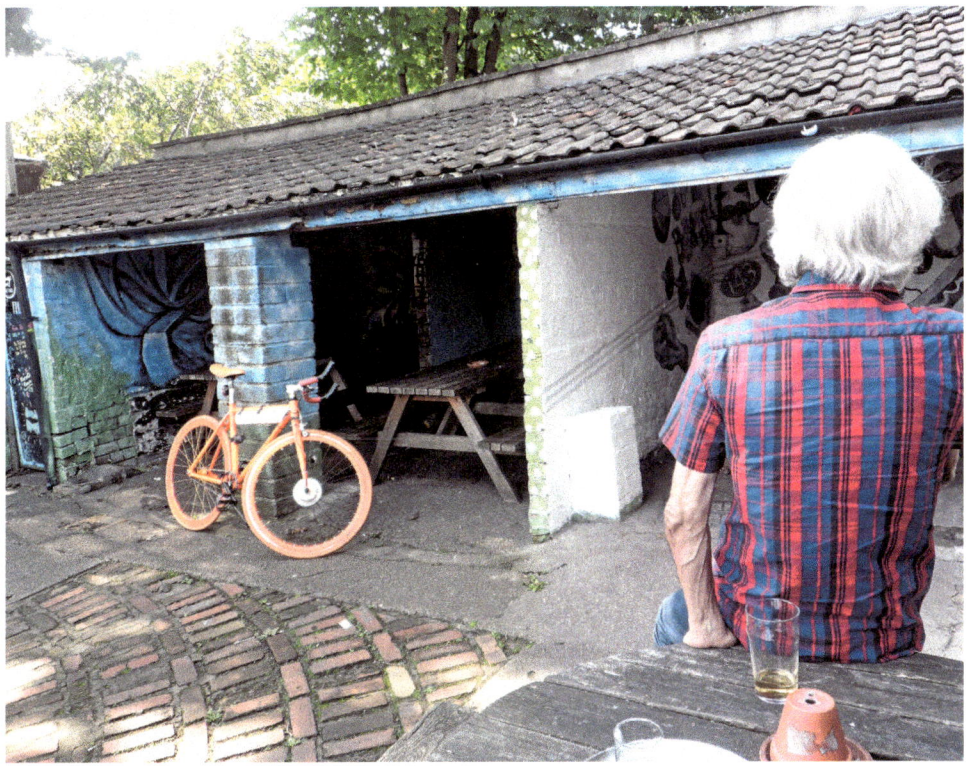

The former pigsties.

cause one or the other to emerge from murky, unknown regions of the pub, Bill with a fag stuck to his bottom lip as he shakily pulled your pint, Gladys's cracked and powdered cheeks wobbling as she attempted a gap-toothed smile. It was like being served by vampires, and we young ones joked that the Grubbs spent their daylight hours lying on Gro-bags in the cellar.

Now that my planned weekend in Bristol has extended to forty years and I'm an old fogey myself, the pub has been officially renamed The Farm and is an altogether brighter, airier place than the one I knew. A summer breeze of urban regeneration has blown away the area's air of dereliction and brought a younger, more discerning clientele to the pub. The waste ground that once surrounded it, formerly part of that long-forgotten farm, really is a farm now, a thriving City Farm run by earnest volunteers dedicated to recycling and the reuse of finite resources.

The best of luck to them, says this old fogey.

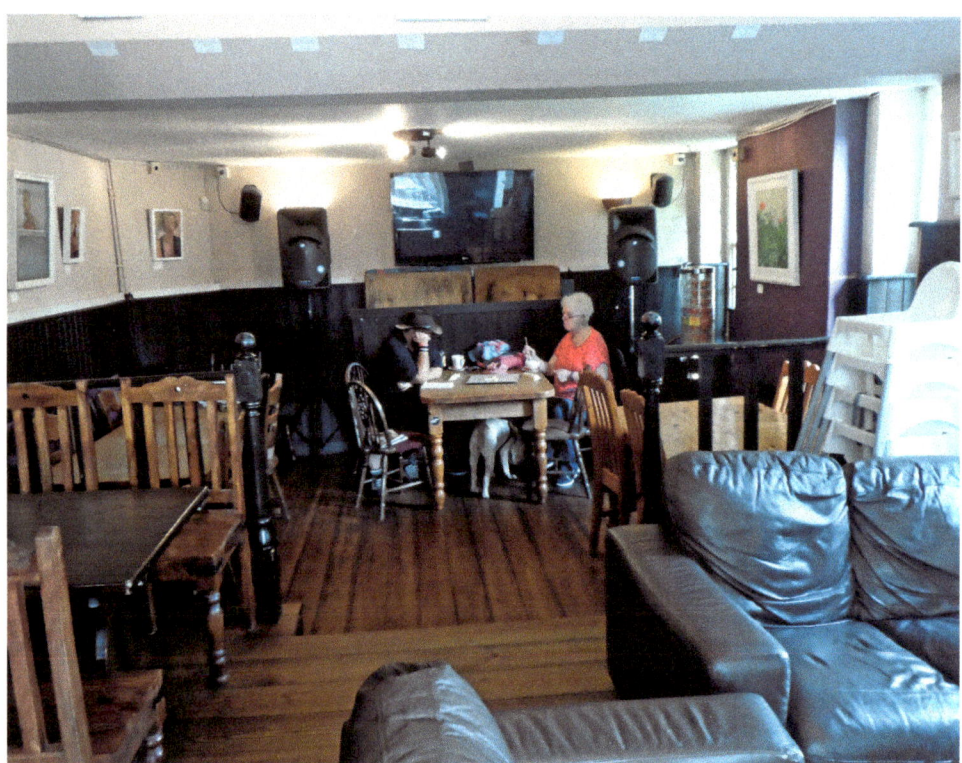

A quiet moment at The Farm.

5

West

39. The Angel, Long Ashton
To those Long Ashton residents who throw their hands up in horror at being included in a book with 'Bristol' in its title, I can only point out that for centuries the village was part of the hundred of Hartcliffe-with-Bedminster, an electoral area that was never abolished but whose use gradually died out. Nowadays part of north Somerset, Long Ashton stands on Bristol's south-west doorstep and is lucky enough to contain a number of treasures. The first of these that the visitor encounters is an old coaching

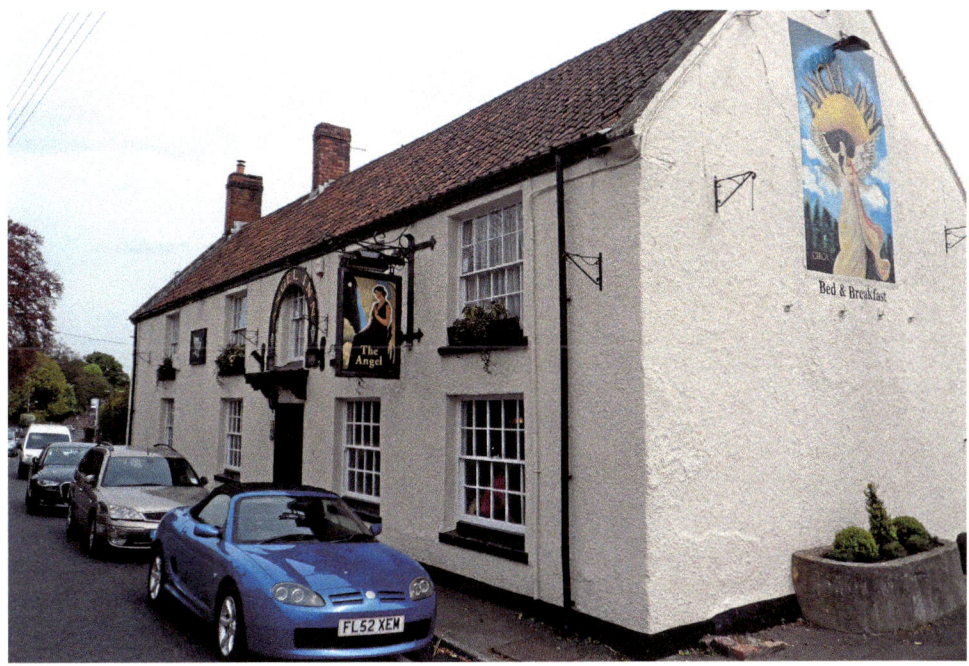

The Angel Inn, Long Ashton.

house, the Angel Inn at the corner of Church Lane, still an inn in the true sense of the word as it offers accommodation to travellers.

Many of Britain's earliest pubs were once religious offshoots, a kind of ecclesiastical outreach that extended into the hospitality sector in medieval times when few people travelled more than a couple of miles from home, and those who did were mainly pilgrims in need of food, drink and stabling for their horses. Monasteries and churches set up houses to cater for their needs, and in this way the ancient All Saints' Church, which stands behind the pub and was built around 1390 on the site of an older church, created the Angel. Incidentally, while many church houses evolved into taverns, others became schools, which is how in eighteenth-century Bristol we had Colston's Hospitall School, and still have the Queen Elizabeth's Hospital school for boys in Clifton. Other church houses took to treating the sick, and eventually morphed into our present hospitals, although in the Middle Ages you rarely got medical treatment at a hospital, what you got was the kind of hospitality still offered by the Angel today.

When the inn was built is uncertain, but it was known as the Church House when it was given to the parish in 1495 by the lord of the manor of Ashton estate, Sir John Choke, as a chantry gift in return for prayers being said for his soul and those of his family. Although the inn only became listed as the Angel in the Directory of 1912, the name is an ancient one, and when the first landlord, Richard Addys, was recorded in 1597 it was probably called the Angel's Visitation. This was more common at the time as it referred to the archangel Gabriel's visit to the Virgin Mary to tell her she was to be the mother of Christ. Seen as a remnant of Catholicism and judged to be politically incorrect when Oliver Cromwell Puritans came to power, the second part of the name was quickly dropped by Angel inns throughout the land.

Not surprisingly as it faces the church, the original entrance door to the Angel was the present back door. Today's front door, too, is certainly very old and will have become the pub's main entrance once the toll road on that side was established as the prime route from Bristol into Somerset. Exactly when this happened is not known, the most likely time was during the 1700s, but although the road has since been superseded, it still gives the Angel its lifeblood of customers. The building is long and fairly narrow, with gabled ends, and retains many of its original features, both inside and out.

Before going into the bar, we may look at the small, cobbled courtyard at the rear. A sign painted on the old stable wall gives the nod to its coaching past by reading, 'GOOD COACHHOUSE & STABLES', and even though this looks a little *too* new, I was heartened to see that it had been restored after research told me that the original sign had been painted over in the late 1970s. The stables also remain, still with saddle-hooks set into the walls but now with tables inside, they are used by drinkers in need of the fresh country air. If there are more relaxing places to sit on a sunny spring day than in the Angel's courtyard, I have yet to find them. Swallows dip and swoop around the building, and it is a small but important touch that the current landlady, Sian Powell, has left the hayloft window open so that they can continue to nest there as they have done since Henry VIII was our country's monarch. The building that stands beside the rear entrance door was one of two small brewhouses at the time when inns made their own beer. They were used for brewing Church Ales, when money was raised for All Saints by holding dances for the village lads and girls.

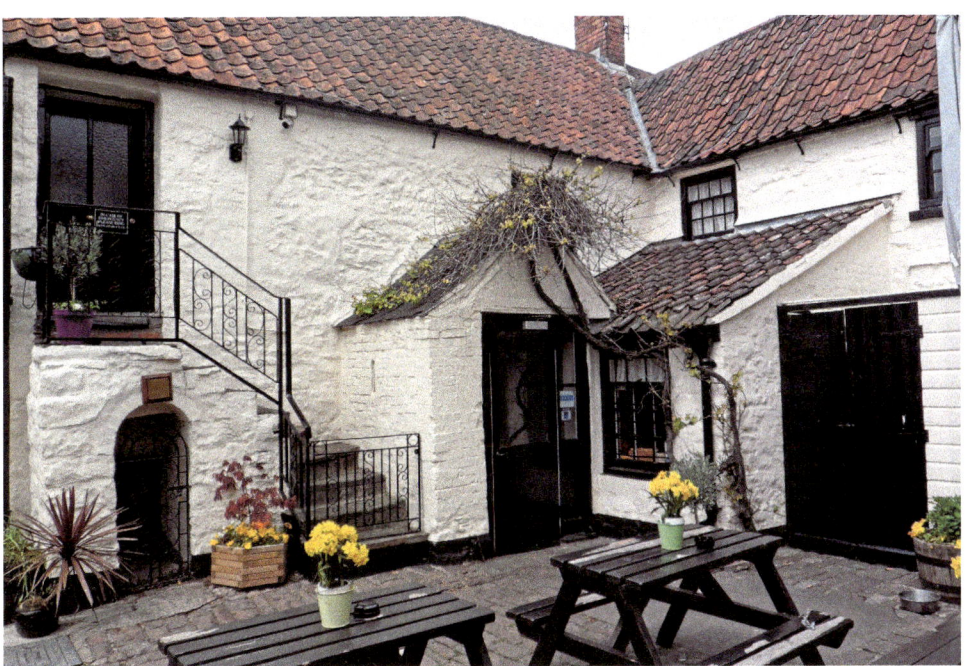

The Angel courtyard.

Inside, the original oak beams are still in place, holding the building together and supporting the roof as they have done for more than five centuries. The heavy oak doors also remain, as do the old wooden window shutters. The Angel caters for a cross-section of society, and you are likely to find yourself next to a farm labourer in muddy wellies, a well-heeled oldie taking his wife out to lunch, or a brace of entrepreneurs discussing business. The stone fireplace, rediscovered behind plaster in the early 1980s when the interior of the building was altered from three separate rooms into one long one, provides a focus for the bar as well as a welcome source of heat on wintry days. In the smoke room there is a late nineteenth-century photograph showing a Long Ashton elder beside the village cross, which stood outside the pub until the road was widened in the last century, when it was moved into All Saints' churchyard.

In olden times, this end of the inn was used as a court presided over by local justices. This use for a public house is not unusual: in 1770 the inquest of the Bristol boy poet, Thomas Chatterton, was held at a London inn before his corpse was flung into quicklime to hasten its disappearance. What is unique about the Angel is that the cellar beneath it was used as a holding prison for offenders, a fact now commemorated by a brass plaque over the entrance from the courtyard. The doorway is small and cramped, the kind of reminder we often see in old buildings of how much bigger people are now than they were in ancient times. Inside the cellar itself there are cell spaces in the walls that were hewn out of the rock, one with an iron ring set into the stone that must have been used to restrain unruly prisoners. For obvious reasons the cellar is not open to the public, but the landlady kindly let me and my twelve-year-old daughter Maria descend

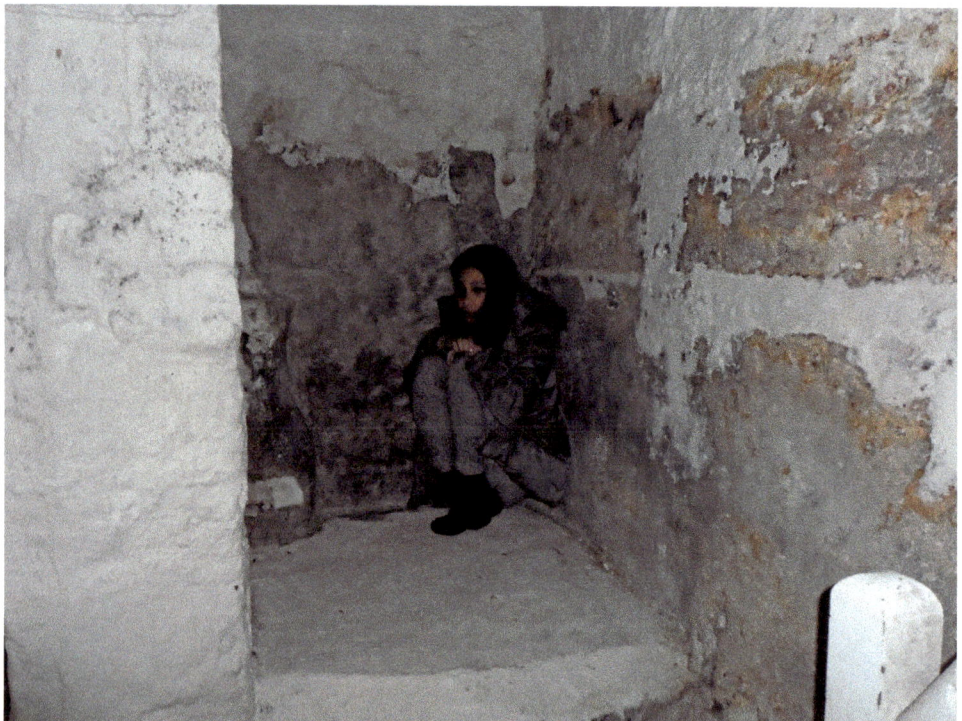

Angel cell.

through the trapdoor, fitted behind the bar in later years, to take a look. To stand in that lonely place and stare at the spaces cut into the walls, where prisoners had to sit in total darkness sometimes for days on end, was strange, eerie and disconcerting.

Beside the inn in Church Lane there is a stone horse-trough, now filled with flowering plants, a relic of the days before the invention of motor transport when horses clattered in and out of the courtyard and farmers held markets there. A few paces further up the lane there stands a small house with distinctive Gothic windows and door, above which there is a plaque informing the reader that this was the village schoolhouse in 1818. It would be a shame to leave Long Ashton without looking at All Saints' Church. At the end of the lane you practically pass through a farmyard to reach it, and on the tower wall you will see the arms of Thomas de Lyons who founded it. As is often the case, there was an earlier church on the spot and two stone figures from this, dated 1280, lie in the porch, one with a dog curled up at his feet to indicate faithfulness. Inside, the ornate tomb of Sir Richard Choke, de Lyons' successor as lord of the manor, is thought to date from 1483. The late medieval rood screen is the best example of its type in England.

One aspect of All Saints that is easily overlooked, literally, is the view from its far side. Unchanged for centuries but for cars moving along a distant road, the rolling Somerset hills stand as they have always done, with fields dotted here and there with sheep and lonely farmhouses shyly tucked away as though hiding from the hurly-burly of twenty-first-century life.

40. Nova Scotia, Cumberland Basin

This unpolished diamond of a dockside pub was purpose built as a hotel in 1811, two years after the floating harbour was completed, to provide accommodation for buyers and sellers when Cumberland Basin was the focal point of the Irish cattle trade. At that time, the archway led to a much larger stable yard and the buildings on the right, which are far older, were stables for the traders' horses with the stable boys housed in the rooms above. The bay window on the pub's extreme left was once the frontage of another inn, the Docks Hotel, which was absorbed into the Nova Scotia in 1898, and during the course of my research I found yet another, the Jolly Sailor, described as being on 'Nova Scotia Wharf'. As there was little or no street lighting in the early nineteenth century, the Nova Scotia Hotel had a large lamp outside to guide visitors to its door, and its original lamp-holder is still there, extending 1.5 metres (5 feet for the old fashioned) over the pavement. Another example of such an arrangement that has survived in Bristol is the one outside the Llandoger Trow and, like that one, the Nova Scotia's has now gained from the fitting of an authentic-looking replica lamp. The pub has retained its original windows, and its outside appearance can have changed little in more than two centuries.

Thankfully, the Nova Scotia's interior has also escaped the modernisation or theming so beloved of breweries nowadays, and has retained intact the atmosphere of an old sailors' haunt. At some point in its history its walls were papered with old sea charts and they remain today, yellowed with time and generations of nicotine from the

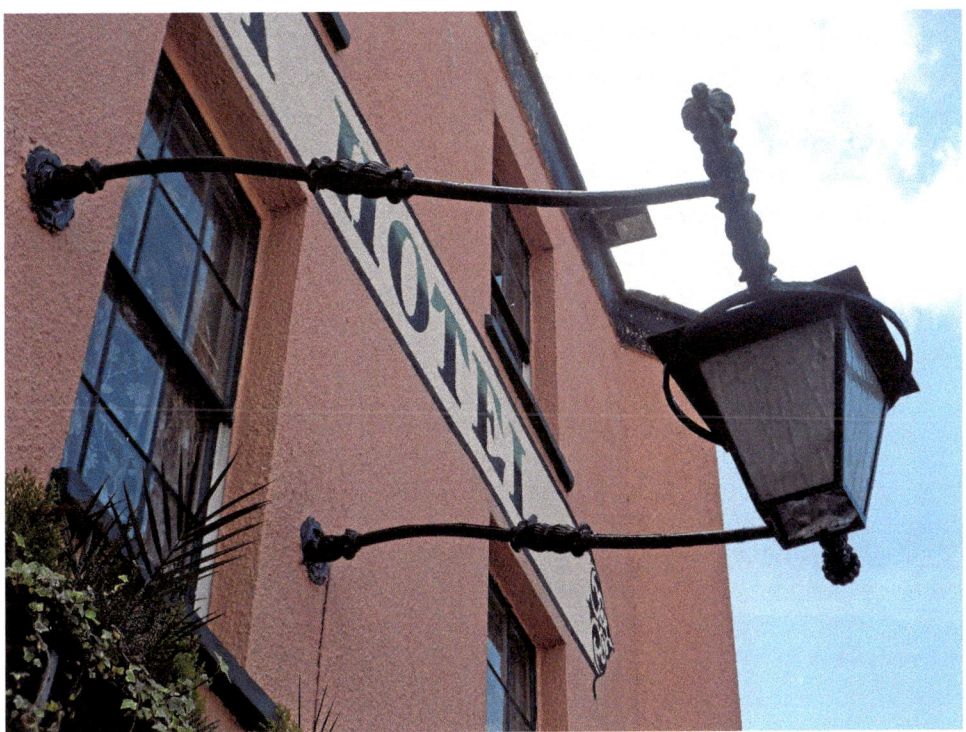

Nova Scotia lamp holder.

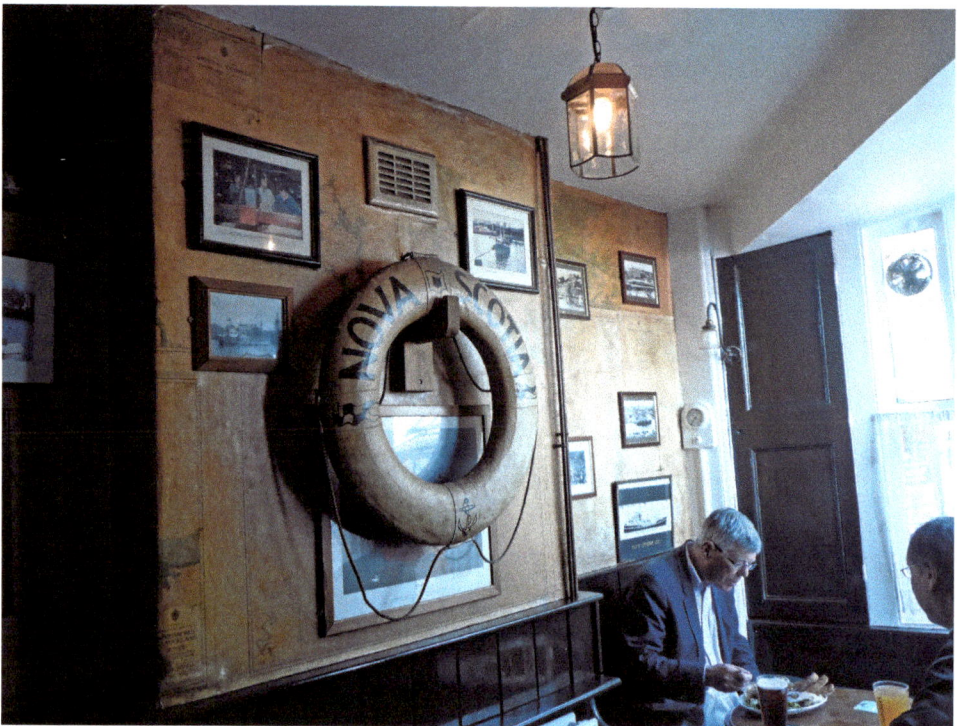

The snug at the Nova Scotia.

bad old days when tobacco was the recreational drug of choice. Old photographs of paddle steamers and the city docks in their heyday cover the walls, where old gas-light brackets remain untouched. The original wooden shutters are still in use and in the delightful little Snug there is an authentic *Nova Scotia* life ring, leftover from the days when part of a dockside pub's duty was to rescue inebriated customers who had staggered over the harbour wall. The mahogany bar, carved by a local carpenter, was originally intended for a ship but it did not fit in its intended home so ended up instead in the Nova Scotia, no doubt at a bargain price for the landlord.

There are tables outside the Nova Scotia where customers can enjoy a drink as they watch sail boats passing and admire the quaint row of Dock Cottages on the far side of the Basin, built by the Port of Bristol twenty years after the pub to house retiring employees. There, if they are especially lucky, they might see the bridge swinging – literally – into action.

Let's hope that this spirited little pub continues to thrive as it has done since its construction.

41. The Avon Gorge Hotel, Sion Hill

The Avon Gorge Hotel is just what it says above its swishy entrance arch – a hotel – but there's a pub within it called the White Lion that is open to the public, and this book would not be complete without including it. To leave it out would be to ignore

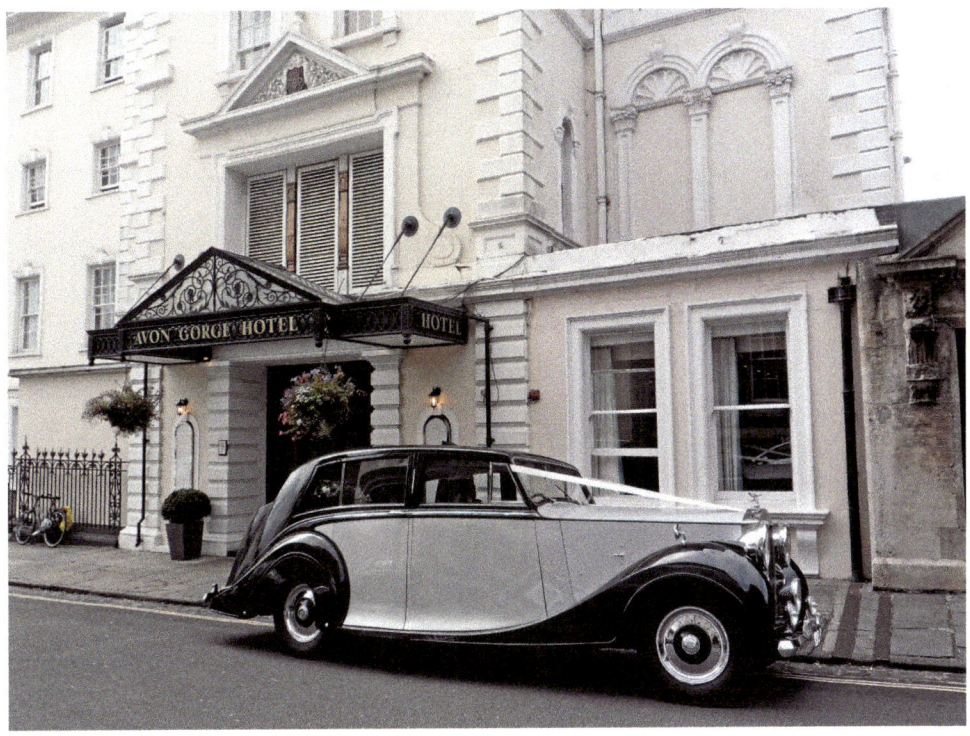

Above: The Avon Gorge Hotel.

Below: View from the terrace.

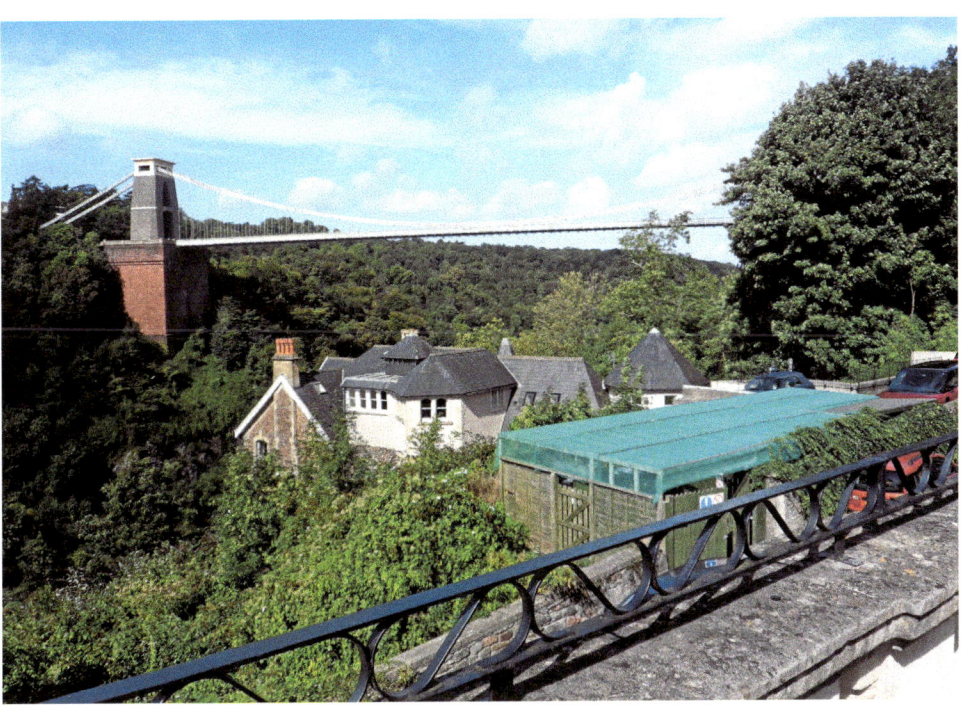

the Avon Gorge's most splendid feature, the spacious terrace from where you can enjoy a drink or something to eat as you look down at the Gorge and the green hills of Somerset beyond. The view is dominated by Isambard Kingdom Brunel's suspension bridge, as strong as it is graceful. As you marvel at it you may recall the Second World War wing commanders who once stood there to raise a glass to rookie RAF pilots, flying under the bridge to show off their bravado and their skill.

The Avon Gorge Hotel was known as the Grand Spa when it opened in 1898. It served visitors to the Royal Clifton Spa next door, which was patronised by the wealthy people and aristocrats who came to enjoy the waters pumped up from their source below in Hotwells. Alas, soon afterwards the warm spring water began to diminish to the trickle it is today, still just about visible at low tide in the River Avon's mudbanks off the Portway. The buildings were put to other uses and stand a stone's throw from Clifton village with its shops, restaurants, pubs and bars.

42. The Coronation Tap, Sion Place

In an age when pub names are changed as often as panties in a Thai brothel, this historic cider house is justifiably proud of having kept the same name for over two centuries. Records before 1839–47, when John Morris was landlord, are sketchy or non-existent, but the present Georgian building is certainly older. The Clifton area

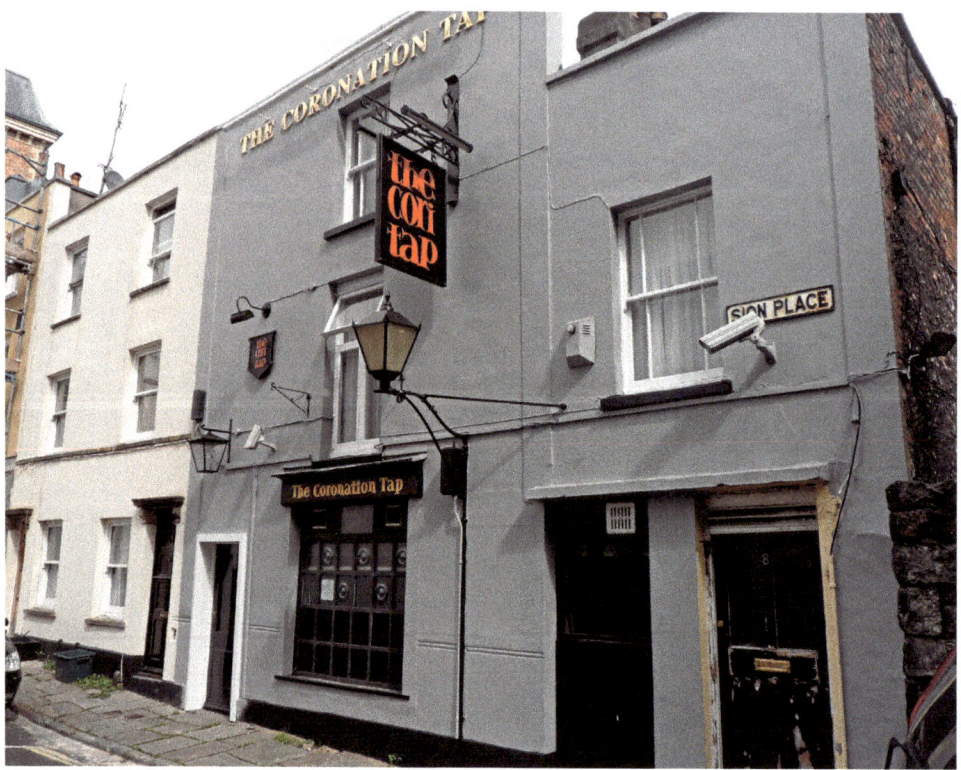

The Coronation Tap.

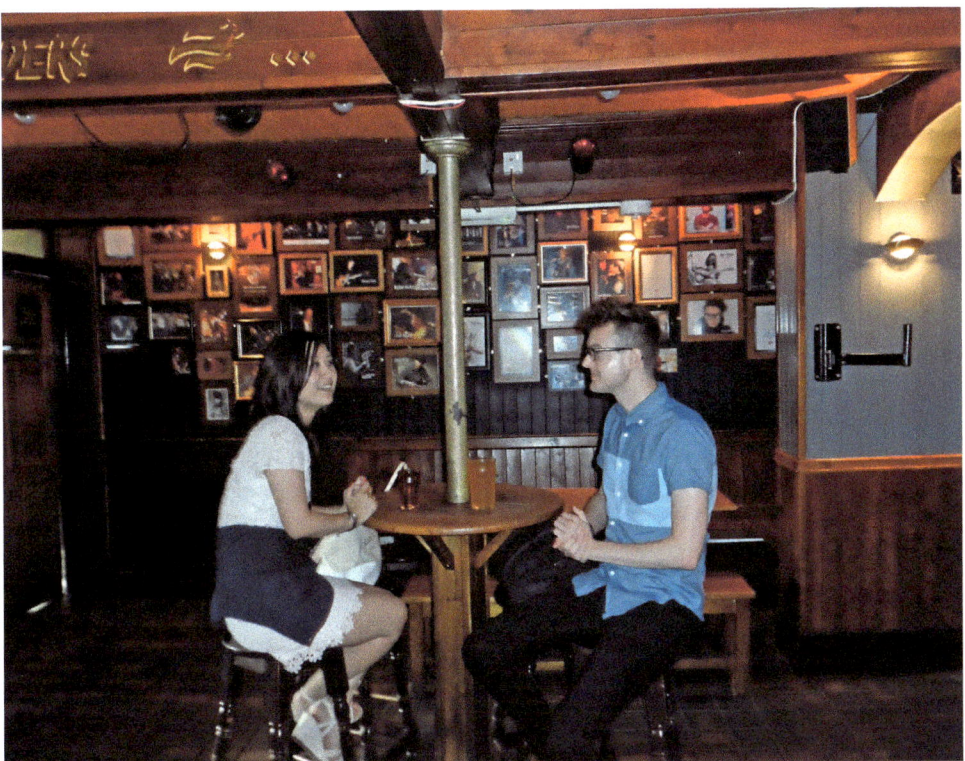

Inside the Cori.

was not developed until the second half of the eighteenth century, before which it was an area of farms and fields that grew food for the nearby walled city of Bristol, and there is evidence that a precursor of the Coronation Tap stood on the same spot, a farmhouse surrounded by orchards selling apples, which evolved gradually into the cider house we know today. Although the Cori, as the pub is known locally, now also sells beer, wines and spirits, it retains its focus on the ancient West Country drink. It sells a range of ciders – all good – but most notably its very own exclusive Exhibition brand, sold only in half pints because of its prodigious strength of 8.4 per cent.

Like the Hole in the Wall pub, the Coronation Tap has entrances in two streets: Sion Place and Portland Street. Its closeness to the University of Bristol makes it a favourite haunt of students but its clientele includes locals of all ages, as well as cider connoisseurs who come from far and wide to worship at its altar. The Cori is also a famed West Country music venue where many of today's stars once played, including Devon soul diva Joss Stone and jazz saxophone maestro, Andy Sheppard. The pub has not always had the convivial atmosphere for which it is now famous. In the 1960s, a now legendary landlord, Dick Bradstock, became so concerned about the rowdy reputation of cider houses that he tried to improve the drink's image by imposing draconian rules. Scruffy clothing was banned and would lead to immediate expulsion, as would asking for a pint for a woman. Snogging earned the same punishment, even when it involved a married couple!

43. The Albion, Clifton

The Albion is so obviously an old coaching inn that to walk the short, cobbled road that leads into its courtyard from Boyce's Avenue is to enter a time-slip that can carry the imagination back to mail coaches, postilions and hansom cabs. When I moved to Bristol in the mid-1970s the stables were still there, on both sides of the pub courtyard, used for storage but leaving no doubt about their original use: by peering in through the cracked and grimy windows you could see the cobbled interior floors, and make out the remains of horses' stalls and feed boxes. There was even the shell of an old handpump outside with a shallow moat beside it to take away the water when the stalls were hosed down. In those days, the Albion had a faded and tatty air about it, with paint peeling from the fractured render on the outside walls and dandelions headbutting their way up between cracks in the courtyard flagstones. It was very much a local, frequented by all strata of the area's residents, including those mysterious males who were common in Clifton in those days; neither old nor young, dressed in jeans that concertina'd around their ankles, usually a scuffed leather jacket and with hair in need of a wash.

The ability of pubs to adapt and slip into the different mantles presented to them by urban decay and renewal never fails to fascinate, and the Albion has undergone a radical change. The exterior courtyard will always be a favoured suntrap in the summer months and its original flagstones remain, but though the stables are a thing of the past the Lantern Room now opens out to bring this delightful outside space into the pub. The bar has a blazing fire in winter, attracting locals as well as well-heeled customers

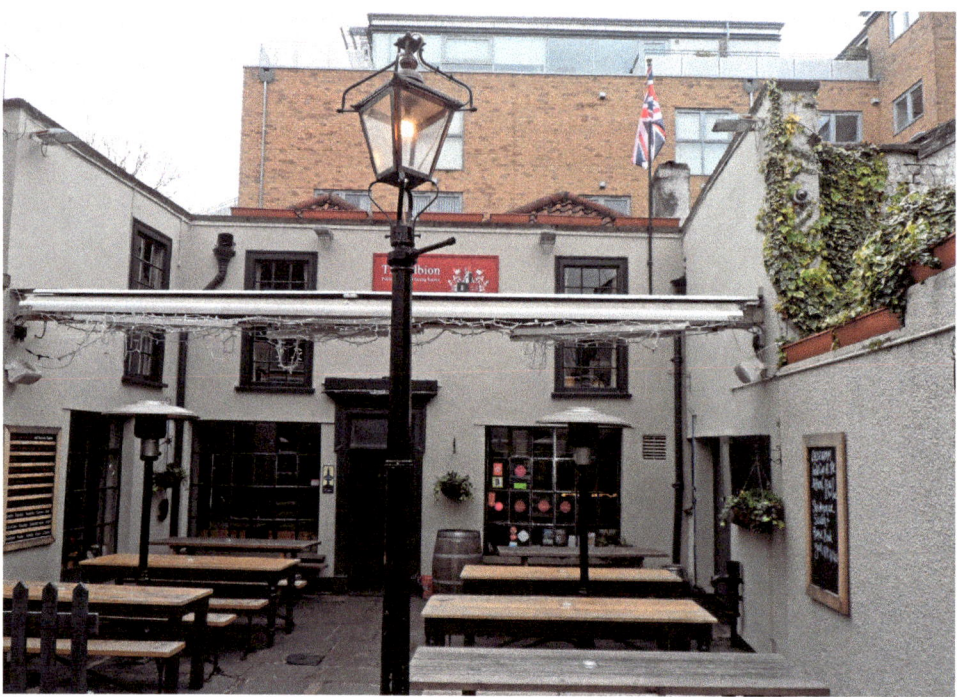

The Albion.

in need of refreshment after leaving the Victorian splendour of the Clifton Arcade or the antique shops and boutiques that pepper Boyce's Avenue and nearby Princess Victoria Street. The date when the Albion was built is unknown. The pub claims to be of seventeenth-century vintage but this is probably a little too early and may refer to an earlier building on the site. In all likelihood the inn was built in the 1770s, either directly by Thomas Boyce or as a result of his efforts to popularise the area that lies around it.

A successful manufacturer of periwigs in King Street, Boyce branched out into property towards the end of the eighteenth century, taking advantage of the growing popularity of the Hotwells Spring, which brought visitors flocking to the general area and created a demand for accommodation. Although it already had a few grand houses, Clifton was still very much a village at that time and to this day the Albion retains some of the atmosphere of a village pub. Boyce built the three large houses that stand to the right of the Albion to cater for the wealthy tourists, describing them in advertisements in 1772 as 'large and elegant lodging houses'. They were probably designed by the Bristol stonemason and architect Thomas Paty, many of whose wonderful buildings survive. They had shops added to their ground-floor fronts many years later, and as a result they are easily missed. Their elegance is undiminished and can be seen to best advantage from the nearby end of Princess Victoria Street.

Unfortunately for Thomas Boyce, his property venture proved too ambitious for his finances and he became bankrupt the following year in 1773. The exact date when the Albion was built remains a mystery, but it may have been a little later and 1778 is a likely date. A 200-tonne ship called the *Albion*, built in the Bristol dockyards and launched that year, was very much in the news at the time and the pub may have been named after her.

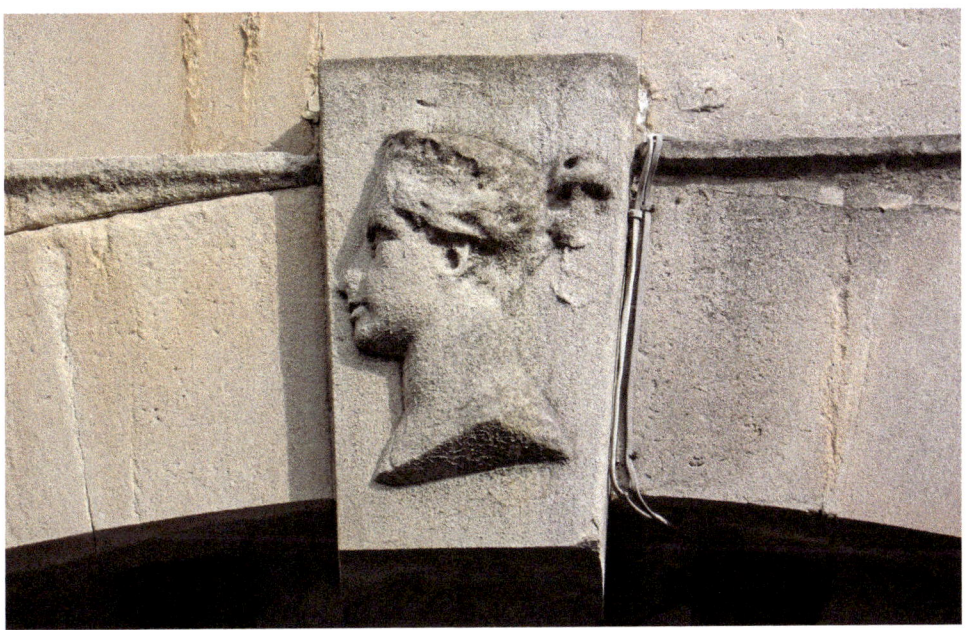

Queen Victoria's portrait.

The archway to the left of the Albion is worth a closer look. Building on the arch, which has a house above it that is now used as a delicatessen, began in 1837. At the highest point of the arch there is a sculpted portrait of the young Queen Victoria. Recently refurbished, this is the same view of the queen in profile that was used on the world's first postage stamp, the penny black.

44. The Lansdown, Clifton Road

Like the Albion, the Lansdown has undergone refurbishment in recent years. All too often this can mean a loss of character, but as one who frequented the pub in the 1980s, when it was tatty and smelled damp, your author can assure you that here refurbishment actually meant improvement. A dog-friendly place, the Lansdown has kept not only its Victorian gas lamps, but also the welcoming atmosphere for which it has long been famous. With the University of Bristol close by, students naturally make up a large proportion of its clientele, but it's also a true local, a community boozer that provides a watering hole for all Clifton residents and visitors without discrimination, so that its customers are an interesting mix. The Lansdown does excellent food, with Sunday roasts a perennial favourite, has a good range of beers including local brews, and possesses a partly covered garden that is heated in winter, where film nights are held *al fresco*. There are cabaret nights featuring everything from circus to magic acts to poetry readings, and on quiz night the landlord actually awards points for heckles, provided they get a laugh.

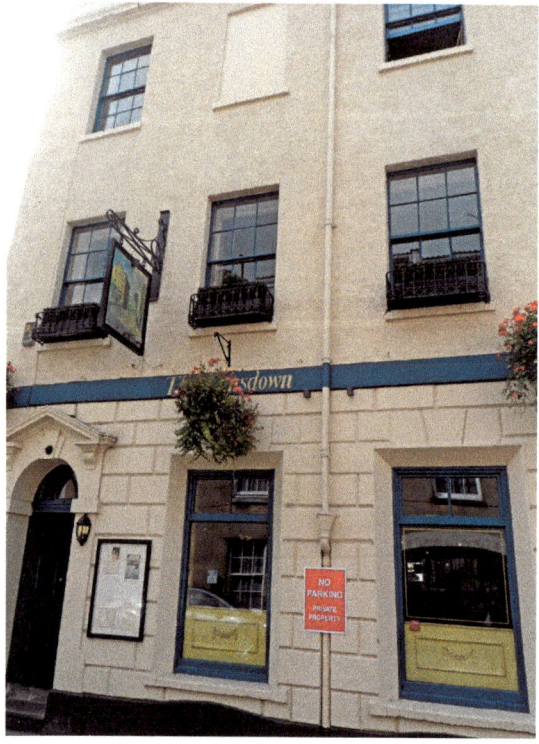

The Lansdown.

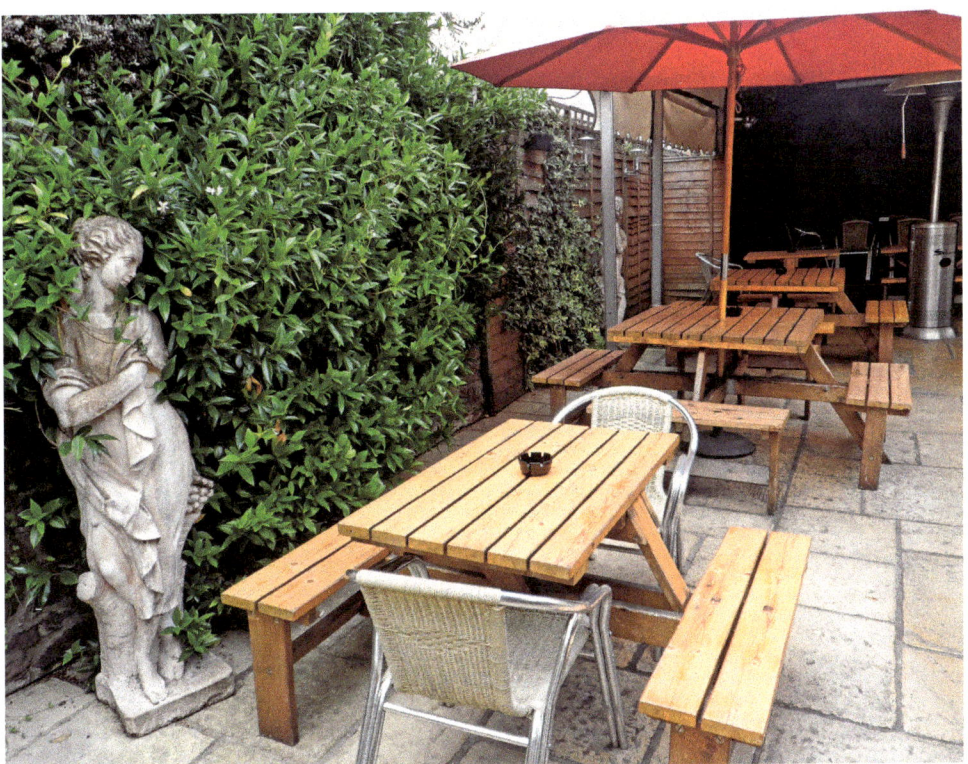

The Lansdown garden.

Originally the Lansdown Hotel, Samuel Verender kept the pub in 1833 and it was still in his family twenty years later when his daughter Emma ran it. A quick glance at the gable end will show that five windows there were bricked up, and it seems likely that this was a result of the prohibitive Window Tax, which remained in force until 1851. In 1861, a scruffily dressed French Canadian, Thomas Lefevre, was charged with stealing a pencil case worth 1s (5p) from the landlord, Welsh-born Mr George. When confronted he handed it back, but George must have pressed charges because Lefevre was bound over to keep the peace at the Police Court, after explaining that he had been very drunk and saying he could not remember the incident.

45. The Lamplighters, Shirehampton

There has been a landing place from the River Avon at the spot now dominated by this beautifully restored old inn since time immemorial. William of Orange, the same king whose face appears on the sign of the Kings Head, made landfall here from Ireland after the Battle of the Boyne in 1690, and travelled onwards to the home of Sir Robert Southwell at nearby Kings Weston House. From ancient times, too, a ferry service, referred to locally as 'the passage', ran to and from the tidal inlet at Crewkerne Pill on the far side of the River Avon. To cater for the needs of travellers, there was an inn known as the Old Passage House beside the spot where the Lamplighters now stands.

The ferry received its death knell with the opening of the M5 bridge over the Avon, and finally gave up the ghost in 1973.

The Lamplighters is not a unique pub name but it is certainly very unusual, and the way the Bristol pub came to be so named is unlikely to have happened elsewhere. It was called Lamplighter Hall when it was built, probably in 1768, by one Joseph Swetman, a tin plate manufacturer of Bristol. Swetman had achieved prosperity when he secured the contract for supplying street lighting for around half of Bristol's parishes. Gas lighting was still in the future and the lamps, doubtless manufactured at his works in Small Street, were run on oil that he also supplied, along with wicks. It seems likely that Joseph Swetman was the son of James Swetman, landlord of the Three Ships' Lanterns on Bristol Back, not only because the name is so unusual, but also because James is described in contemporary sources as 'a tinman'.

Despite his background in the victualling trade, Swetman did not open Lamplighter Hall as an inn, he built it as his home in retirement, adding a marvellous balcony so that he could look out over the river and enjoy the view of Pill. The invention of the balcony has been credited to Lord Arundel, and there was one in London's Covent Garden in 1659 'which country folk were wont to gaze on'. The fashion must have

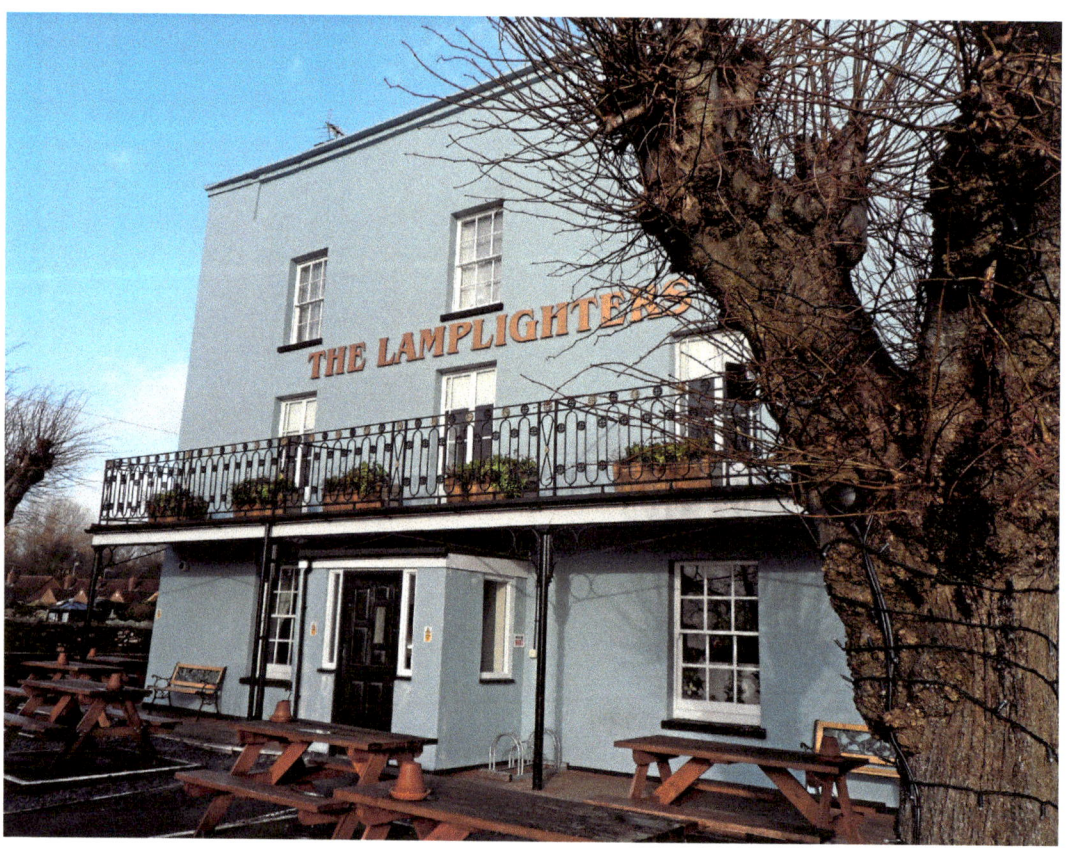

The Lamplighters.

been well established in Bristol by the time Swetman added his iron structure to the front of Lamplighter Hall. Listed now so that it cannot be demolished or altered, the balcony complements the classic eighteenth-century proportions of the building beautifully. Unfortunately for Joseph Swetman, though, the smell of the Avon's 'brackish water' as it carried Bristol's sewage out to sea did not agree with him, and he moved elsewhere. He is thought to have died in 1772 and his home, sold two years later, then became an inn.

Driving along the Portway in the past, I often noticed a street sign – Hung Road – and wondered how it came about. A memorial to some particularly well-endowed resident, perhaps? The answer to the riddle has a tenuous link to the Lamplighters. The inn's association with the sea has always been close, and in the days of sail there were two anchorages or 'roads' where ships sheltered while they waited to enter Bristol, or to be cleared at the custom house at Pill. Kingroad was near the mouth of the river while Hungroad, which probably gained its name because moored ships hung there at the end of chains, was close to the Avon's Horseshoe Bend at Shirehampton. Due to congestion in the port, as well as adverse weather and the huge tidal range of the river, the second largest in the world that can raise or lower water levels by 14 metres, ships often had to wait for long periods, and this brought trade to the Lamps, as the pub is known locally.

In March 1793, a Captain Samuel Kelly was lying at Pill in his brig, *Mayflower*, when he was visited by a privateer, Captain Duckett, anchored in the Kingroad, who prevailed upon him to dine at Lamplighter's Hall with another privateer, Captain John Shaw. Afterwards Captain Kelly said, 'I cannot say I was highly entertained with the conversation, it being in a style I much disliked.' This is hardly surprising in a law-abiding seafarer like Captain Kelly. Duckett had achieved notoriety operating out of the Iles de Los off the slave coast of Guinea in his ship *General Ord*, of fourteen guns and fifty men, while Captain Shaw, Haven master of Hungroad, was known as 'the bold privateer' after his ship, *Lion*, with forty-four guns and 168 men, had engaged the French vessel *L'Orient* in the Bay of Biscay, and beaten her seventy-four guns and 800 men in a two-hour battle. Captain Shaw's obelisk can be seen today, much overgrown, in the graveyard of nearby St Mary's Church.

The Lamplighters was also a favourite haunt of the pilots based at Pill. They were a feisty bunch and they had to be, as they gained their work by sailing out into the Bristol Channel where they competed for ships, with the first one to hail a merchantman gaining the pilotage. They were employed by the Merchant Venturers, who often found them difficult to control. In November 1793, for instance, when a committee turned up at Lamplighter Hall to examine the pilots, some were told off for being drunk, while others began fighting in front of their visitors. Not all events at the Lamplighters were so acrimonious, though. When the Bristol Freemasons dined there the following year, 'a Brotherly Dinner and Good Wine kept the Brethren till late, but all parted in good order'. Other regulars at the inn were the watermen who towed seagoing ships to and from the port of Bristol with rowing boats. In 1836, more than twenty Pill men attacked the Avon's first steam tug, the *Fury*, as she lay anchored at Portishead, and the watermen of Pill were still using muscle to tow ships fifty years later. In 1886, they

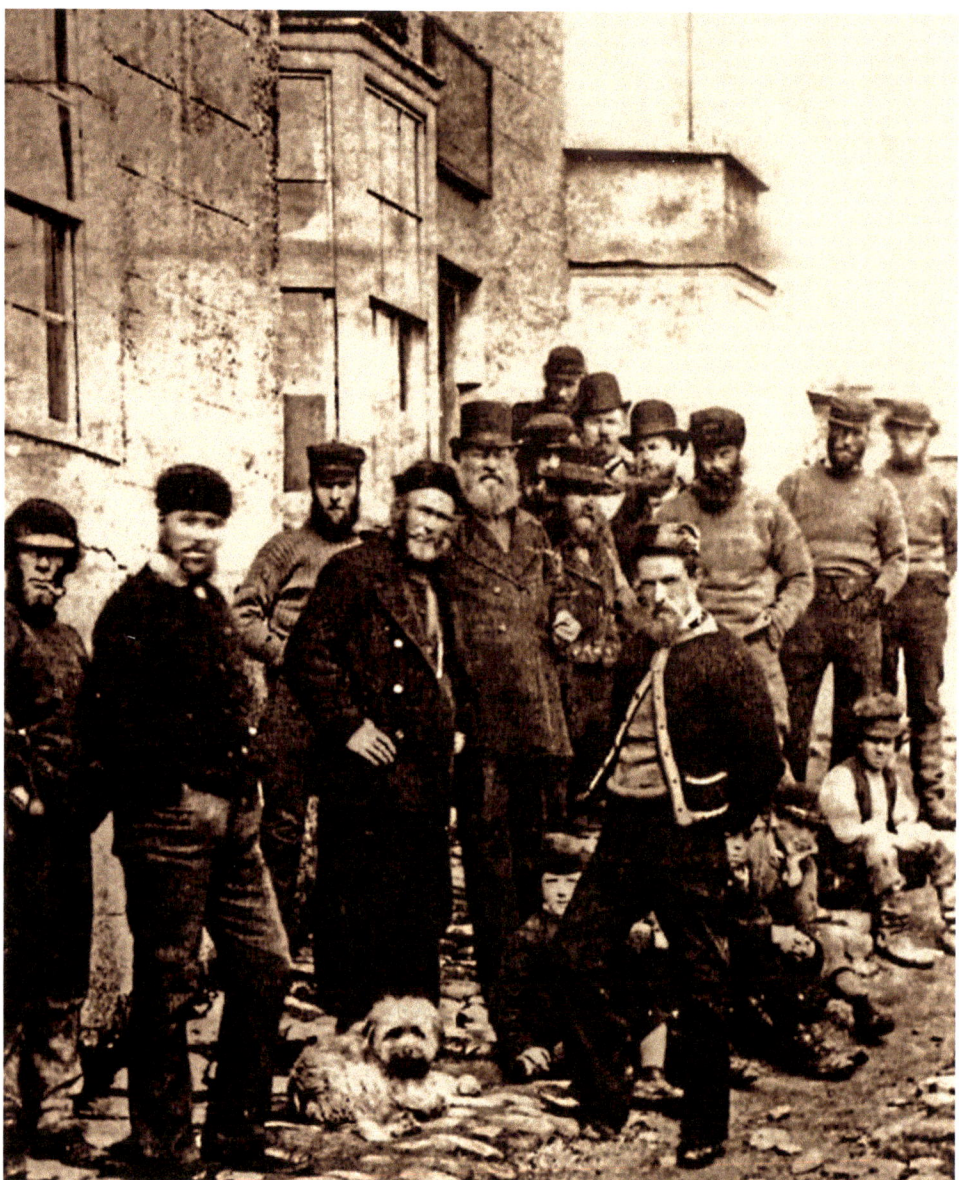

Pill pilots, *c.* 1880.

charged 4*d* (around 2p in today's coinage) per ton for towing ships from Bristol to Avonmouth, while the towage to Newport or Cardiff cost double that amount.

In 1782, a return coach service from the Bush Inn in Corn Street was introduced for passengers travelling to and from ships on the Avon and a ferry that ran to Somerset, and this proved popular for decades. Passage Road became Lamplighter's Hall Road in 1847 but the change was short-lived: when Shirehampton railway station opened in 1865 it took its present name of Station Road. Standing alone at the end, with only the Bristol Sailing Club keeping it company as it has done for more than two centuries,

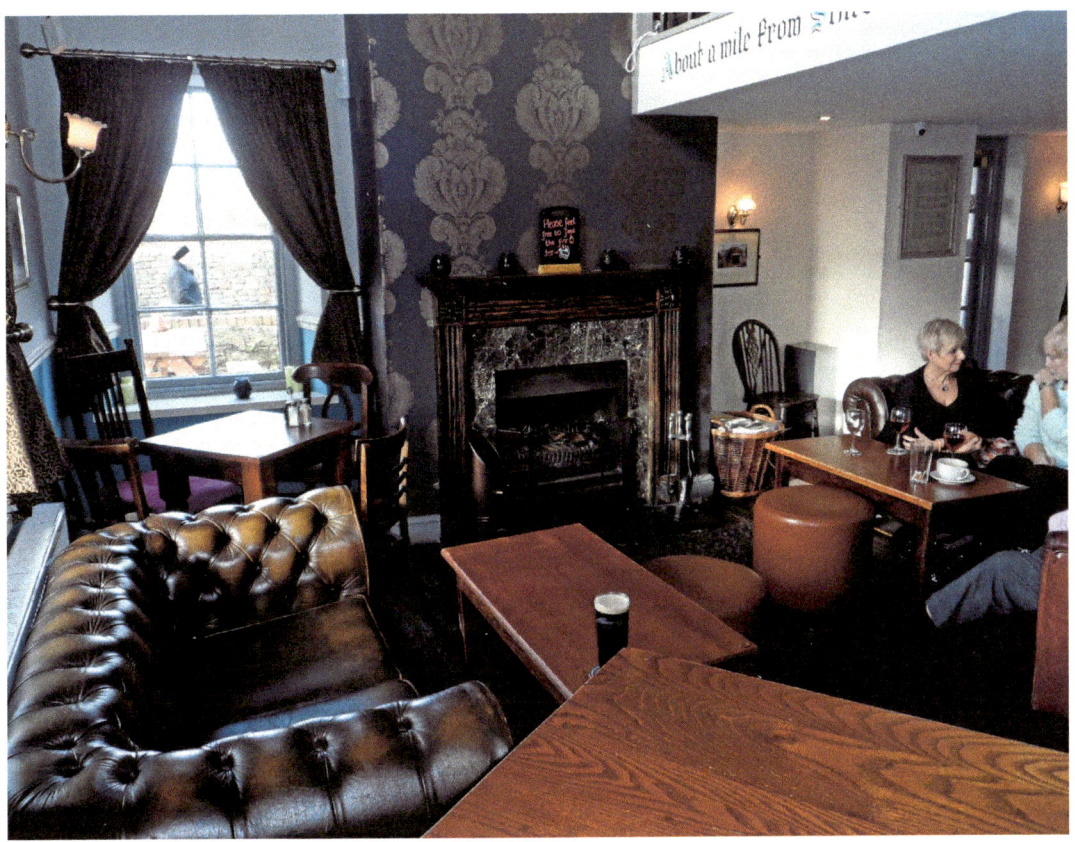

The Lamplighters lounge.

the Lamps could feel isolated but there is no doubting its popularity. When it closed in 2009 the sight of its boarded-up windows spurred Shirehampton residents and local businesses into action, and with the backing of MP Charlotte Leslie a campaign was launched to save it. This was achieved when it reopened in 2011, restored to its former glory with new sash windows, iron balustrades and a circular window by the bar.

You can't keep a good pub down.

Acknowledgements

For images, the late Derek Fisher.

With thanks to the following sources
Dening, C. F. W., *Old Inns of Bristol*, (1943).
Eason, Helena, *Bristol's Historic Inns* (1982).